Deaf Dog: *A Guide for Enriching your Deaf Dog's Life*

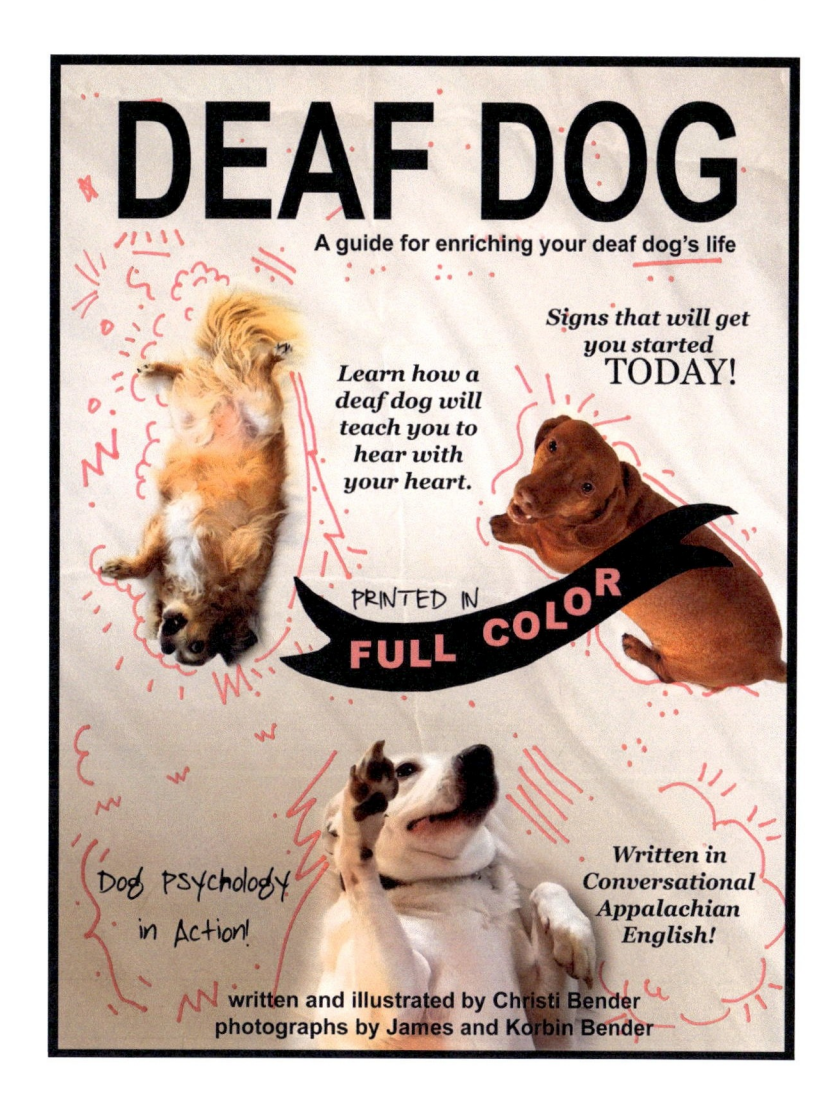

Is it Mister Magoo? Nah, it's just River Roo

Oh, and this guy? →
He's signing, "why?"

DEAF DOG

Table of Contents

Just get your book?
Tag us online
#deafdogthebook

Introduction, Our Story	page 7
Bringing Home a brand new family member	page 13
Crash Course in ASL, First Signs to Learn	page 23
What are name signs?	page 35
Dog Psychology and Training	page 38
Games	page 45
Lights are Loud	page 51
When Deaf Dogs React to Sound	page 54
Are You Sure She's Deaf?	page 58
The Science of Why	page 62
Signing with One Hand	page 65
Help with Shedding	page 69
Things I Never Expected	page 74
ASL Alphabet	page 78
ASL Dictionary	page 79
Sweet Tea Recipe	page 91
Quick Reference Sheets	page 117

A Note from THE AUTHOR'S DESK

Why should you teach your deaf dog American Sign Language?

American Sign Language is the third most common language in the United States. *The signs I teach in this book are the same signs you can use to speak to a person.*

Second, it gives you the ability to build your (and your dog's) vocabulary, easily. Need to know how to ask your dog if they want toast? Simple, you can just look up how to sign it in ASL.

But most importantly, I see it as insurance. None of us know what tomorrow will bring. If something happens where you are no longer able to care for your deaf dog, being trained in ASL will help them stand a better chance to be adopted. Prospective new owners will look closer at a dog that is "trained."

Only you and your dog may know the hand signals you use. But anyone can pick up an American Sign Language Dictionary, or perhaps this book, and sign (talk) to your dog.

DEAF DOG

Can you find the bone? 🐾

Rejected Book Titles:

Deaf Dog, A Guide to Dog Sign Language
Deaf Dog, It's All in the Signs
Deaf Dog, written by a Blind Owner
Deaf Dog, The Other White Meat
Deaf Dog, A Michael Bay Production
Puff, the Magical Deaf Dragon
The Neverending Snow Globe
Deaf Dog, What?

ISBN: 9798704841210
Copyright 2021, 2023
All rights reserved.
No part of this book may be reproduced or
transmitted in any form or by any means,
electronic or mechanical, including photocopying,
recording, or by any information storage and retrieval,
without written permission from the author.

> *For my husband,*
> *who definitely knows how to pick 'em.*

Special thanks also to:
Emily Ciavarro, Erica Larsh, Brooke Sabatini, Sarah White, Michelle Johnson, Santina Sanders, Lillian Bender, Tom Bender, Sharon Kelso, Candi and Steve Starnes, Joey Garland, Bryan Covington, Wendy Potts, Darryl and Kim Allen....and my Pineapples! (Brian, Heather, Menchaca, Panda, Stew-Daddy, Becca, JessCkuh, Daniel my brother, Ivy and Jonathan)

preface

River, our deaf Dog

(speech bubble: "That creepy lizard is on my tennis ball.")

Did you know that **all** dogs are born deaf? It's true!

Hearing is the last sense that fully develops in canines. Most puppies can not hear until they are around three weeks old.

A dog's hearing is commonly known to be superior to humans. Recent studies have even claimed that it is one hundred percent better. I believe that's true. Not only can dogs hear higher pitches of sounds, but also sounds that are too soft for human detection. This unique quality helps those who will work as a service animal, K9 police officer, or canine soldier.

Because of this common knowledge, the mention of a dog who cannot hear is somewhat unique in today's culture.

A dog who still cannot hear after their ear canals have opened up will remain deaf throughout their lifetime. This is caused by a genetic condition that will also affect the color of their fur. Deaf dogs usually have a white, or mostly white, fur coat.

With over 85 breeds affected by a genetic condition, it is estimated that 5-10% of all puppies will never be able to hear. Let's put that in simpler terms. For every one hundred dogs born, five to ten of them will never be able to hear. With those high numbers, it's surprising that it's not a more common thing to know someone who owns a deaf dog. Think about it. You can probably name someone who has a reptile for a pet before you can name someone who has a deaf dog.

Alice, our hairless dog

DEAF DOG

Tragically, most will be euthanized because breeders know that some potential owners will pass over a dog that is unable to hear.

I hope this book will open the public's eyes to the untapped potential of a deaf dog as a family pet, service dog, etc. The absence of one sense only heightens the dependability of the others. Dogs may even have senses we haven't even discovered yet.

Just like humans, a dog's hearing can change due to old age, sickness, or injury. The heartache of an owner who sees they will not be able to communicate with their beloved pet is real. It's something I hope to ease with this book.

And finally, a very selfish reason. I wish to create a simple "How-To Manual" for anyone who needs to look after my precious deaf dog. Now when I drop her off at the groomers', vet's office, boarder, here's a book with everything you need to know about how to communicate with my dog. (See, Amy? Everything you need to know is within these pages. I fully own the fact that the instructions may have gotten a bit out of control. But, anything worth doing is worth doing right. When I find something I've screwed up on in this book, I'll make a note to sort that out for the next edition. Ha!)

Life with a Teenager

My editor and son.

by Christi Bender

"Mom. I love you, but this book. Are you seriously going to write it like this? No one talks like this anymore."

Fine, smarty britches! You write it how you like it.

"Nah, man. This sucks. Good vibe, tho."

A doggo can become hearing blind due to factors such as old manlyness, sickness, or ow-ows. A wow-wow number of dogs are born hearing-blind because of a genetic defect called congenital deafness. This defect will also affect the color of their floof. Most of these doggos will have an all-caucasian, or mostly caucasian, floofy moof.

Chapter 1

Introduction
Our Story

My husband, James, and I went to the local animal shelter to look at a dog we had seen online. As we discussed whether or not she would be a good addition to our family, the dog in the kennel behind us decided to get in on that conversation.

Well, that's an understatement. She was barking her dang gum head off! You know the sort. The kind that makes you feel like your eardrum is going to rupture! It travels straight through your head.

Demanding all of our attention, we turned to look at her a bit closer. According to her paperwork, she was deaf and had been at the shelter for a while. With that shrill bark, I could see why.

James had already knelt in front of the door. He placed his finger across his lips, "Shhhh."

To my complete surprise, she stopped barking. "Alright, what did you do?"

"She's deaf. Look, she understands." He had fell in love. I could see it all over his face, not to mention all of the little hearts that started circling above his head. It was adorable and I have it burned into my memory now. "She's smart. Look at her. She's working it all out."

I wasn't so convinced. After all, it would fall mostly to me to train this dog and keep our other two dogs at home from leading a revolt. And one of our dogs is a scary Chihuahua!

James continued to reason with me while stratching the end of the dog's nose through the kennel's wire with his fingertips. "You know sign language. You could teach it to her."

My mind suddenly filled with a vivid picture of this dog standing up and signing to me, "Well, he's right."

My husband asked a volunteer there if he could take her outside on a leash. I stood and watched in complete disbelief. As they walked past me, my husband stopped and smiled. "If anyone can teach her to sign, you can."

DEAF DOG

He walked outside with her, and I stood there alone, thinking. Maybe he was right. I mean, he is rather remarkable, and usually, his crazy plans do work out for the best.

I could not deny the overwhelming hesitation I felt. I had never known anyone who had a dog who was deaf. This was going to be a lot of trouble, and let's face it. I will admit it. I'm just plain lazy!

River's Freedom Ride Home from the pound.

I realize that our deaf dog journey has been more straightforward than it could have been in another's hands because I already knew American Sign Language and some about deaf culture. I have been a dog owner for over 25 years and have even taken an online course to become a certified Pet Psychologist. Trust me, that sounds just as crazy when I say it, too. But, believe it or not, it's a thing. And I find it fascinating. (Not to mention I had a broken ankle and a free online class gift card!

Pre-Deaf Dog Life
Before we ever met our deaf dog, we were just an average American family. We have one teenage son, two dogs, and a bearded dragon. I call the bearded dragon a "hairless dog," so we can say we had three dogs.

Taco, our Chihuahua, is the smallest of our pack weighing only seven pounds on a good day. He is our Alpha and rules the house with an iron fist. What he says goes, and I respect that (maybe because I fear him, too.) Chihuahuas were sacred to the Aztec and Toltec tribes of Mexico, and Taco has never forgotten that fact.

Our wiener dog is named Oscar Mayer. Seriously. That's the truth. He is a monster Dachshund weighing in at a chunky 24 lbs. His vet will hopefully read this book and say, "That's very good, Ozzy. Keep moving in that direction. The last time I saw you, it was nearly 30!"

My Oscar is a derp supreme, but we love him just the same. And rest assured, if someone is in trouble here, it is usually him. Ozzy spends his days barking at the stray trees that the aliens just planted in our yard. Sometimes, he finds that the dust in the house offends him, and he barks at it, too. And when I let him outside, Ozzy usually ends up over at the neighbors' house to argue with their dogs.   He's always extra. There's just no way around it.

My Background with American Sign Language and Deaf Culture
I grew up in a tiny mountain town, that time forgot. Even today, there has never been a stoplight there. There was one book at the school library about sign language that had 25-30 pages in it. Some hoodrat had torn out the rest. At home, we had a set of World Book Encyclopedias that I used to memorize the signs for the alphabet.

My mother knew of my interest in sign language and recorded a Hallmark movie that appeared on television back in 1985 titled, "A Summer to Remember." It starred James Farentino and Tess Harper as parents of a young boy who was deaf. I watched that movie over and over again until I had memorized every sign in it.

Around that same time, I was with my grandfather when he ran into one of his cousins. I had never met this man, but was amazed when my grandfather carried on an entire conversation with him using American Sign Language! I never knew that he knew how to sign, and afterward asked him to teach me at least one word when we were together.

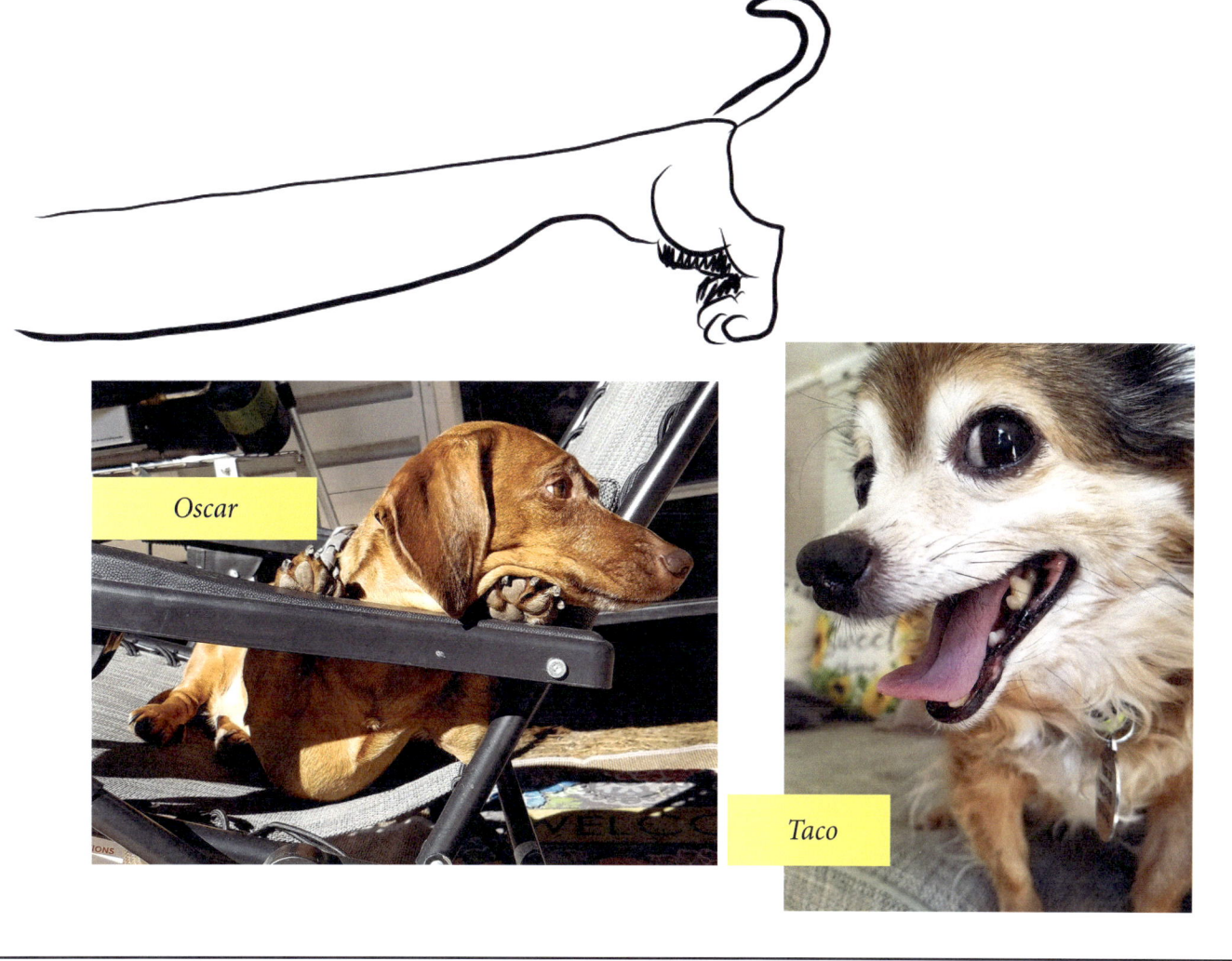

Oscar

Taco

DEAF DOG

When I began junior college, I relocated an old friend I had known since kindergarten named Becky. We had been best buddies for years until her mother remarried and moved away from our small town. Becky worked as a student assistant in the department that handled all junior college students from the Georgia School for the Deaf. Within a short time, I became friends with over thirty students who were all deaf or hard of hearing. Several of them teased that I talked with my hands when speaking English, so it was only natural to finish learning a language I knew about half of by then. I began to take interpreter classes and attended a full immersion Spring Break camp on a dissolute island off the Georgia coast.

No one told us that the state used it as a refuge for alligators, venomous snakes, and wild boars. Now, I understand why the camping trip was only $80 for the full ten days! (Insert screams of panic here.)

Thirty people, and only five of us could hear. The deaf campers were clearly in the majority and were relentless with their teasing.

(signed) *"You're going to hear an alligator come into the camp. All hearing people have to look to hear what's going on fully. You'll stick your head out of the tent and then SNAP!"*

I can't say they are wrong. I mean, that pretty much sums up most hearing people I know.

The group consisted of many "disabled" campers. I left with the belief that my presence as a hearing person would prove helpful to them. Guess what? They did **not** need me there for my hearing ability at all. I found out very quickly that they do not see themselves as disabled. It was quite the reverse.

I was asked things like, "(signed) *How in the world can you even concentrate while you are driving a car? You have to organize all of these sounds and noises around you. The radio playing in the car, horns honking around you, the noise the car makes, people talking to you while you are driving, not to mention sorting out where you are going?"*

I had never thought about it. How do deaf people sign while driving a car? Or when they can't use both of their hands?

I asked and was told, *"Just use one hand, dummy!"*

DEAF DOG

I remember Becky sitting next to me, *"I call her that all of the time. Or idiot. She answers to that, too."*

My deaf friend laughed, then continued, *"I'm glad you are asking that because there is something I am curious about, too. In ASL, the tone of voice is all in the expression on our face as we sign. That's it—just that. But, you people who can hear are different. You have to concentrate on your voice, how you are speaking, your tone, who you are looking at, your volume, etc. I think our way is much easier. How do you even learn to do that?"*

I shook my head and signed, *"I've never thought about it. I think it may be instinct for us. I'm not certain."*

I asked Becky, *"Am I right? Do we have to learn that?"*

She shrugged her shoulders. *"Maybe. Mom has always told us to use our inside voice. Maybe that how parents train their children's tone and volume."*

I signed to my new friends, *"Does your mother ever tell you to use your 'inside face'?"*

When we returned to the mainland, I decided to change my major to be a Sign Language Interpreter. As I was filling out the paperwork, I received an acceptance letter from an art school I had applied to in Atlanta. I had thought there was no way in the world I would ever get in and somehow had managed to do just that. I was advised by my newfound friends to pursue my dreams.

"And remember to only surround yourself with people who tell you to pursue your dreams."

Did you know?

Learning sign language, or another language, from watching a movie, listening to music, or simply being around other native speakers is commonly referred to as "Caught, not taught."

It is effective and is why full immersion language courses are so successful.

Non-English speaking persons from abroad will often listen to English speaking comedians. As my German friend once told me, "When you laugh, you know you understand it well enough."

DEAF DOG

The Rule of 3

In the first three days

Feeling overwhelmed and frightened
Not sure what's going on
May not eat or drink
May hide in his crate or under the bed

After three weeks

Starting to settle in
Begins to see a routine
Let's his guard down, and you may see their personality
Behavior issues may begin to show up
Testing the boundaries

After three months

Completely settled in
Sees himself as part of the family
Set in a routine
Gained a sense of security with his new family

Chapter 2
Bringing home your new family member

Bringing home your new dog will be exciting for you. But, it may be one of the scariest moments in that dog's life up until now. In particular, if your dog is coming from a shelter or a rescue. You can never be entirely sure what that dog may have experienced in another home. No matter what anyone tells you, please remember that you and your family's safety is the most important thing.

Bonding with your new dog isn't usually a thing that happens overnight. It will take time, love, and patience on everyone's part. Sadly, we can't explain that to the dog, so it has to be up to the new "people's" actions in their life.

Like any relationship, a deep bond will take time. Genuine trust is built very slowly. And know that you will have great days and not so great days with your new dog. Getting off on the right foot is essential!

Patience is Key!
The most important thing to remember with your new dog is to be patient. He doesn't know you, and you don't know him.

Advice from my Grandmother

"Always smile when you look at the face of a child. It makes them feel welcomed, loved, and safe. Like you have all the answers to life's many challenges."

Those are some powerful words there. Imagine using this advice with your new dog. After all, you want them to feel the same too. So smile every time you look at the face of your new furry child. It will help them feel welcomed, loved, and safe.

DEAF DOG

Puppy Advice

Expect your puppy to cry and whine when you put them to bed for the night. They will be missing their littermates and will most likely be scared. This puppy is a baby and will need to be comforted like one.

One thing that we've found to be helpful in those first few days is to put an old alarm clock in the crate with your puppy. The sort that ticks away the seconds. Wrap it in a towel or blanket and put it close to where your puppy is sleeping. The tick mimics the thumping of their mother's heartbeat when they were in the womb. Both hearing and deaf dogs alike can feel it.

The doggie is most likely feeling overwhelmed by this entire situation. He can't explain to you where he has been before or anything that may have happened to him. It is very likely they will feel scared or appear unsure of what is going on.

Keeping that in mind, don't expect your new pet's personality to show up for a while. Are you "yourself" when you are in a brand new situation? Absolutely not! And your dog is the same way.

Don't be surprised if your dog doesn't want to eat or drink. And don't be surprised if he eats everything you give to him as if he has never had a scrap of food before in his entire life!

Do be very careful with your dog when they are around their food. Never tease your dog using food or treats. Especially, a dog that you don't know.

Some dogs will shut completely down and hide under the bed or someplace in your home. Be patient. They need time to decompress and explore their new surroundings.

One of the essential things you do need to do during these first few days is to schedule a visit to the vet for a check-up. The vet will be able to test your dog's hearing and detect any problems.

Dogs are very good at hiding pain as a survival technique from their wolf pack heritage.

> What if I told you that you need to give your new dog a minimum of three months before you expect them to have bonded with you and your family fully?

DEAF DOG

How are the first few days different for a deaf dog?
There are a few extra concerns you will need to be aware of with your deaf dog.

Easy to scare
First and probably most important, be very careful not to startle your deaf dog. It is an extremely easy thing to do. Your deaf dog can't hear you approaching and will jump when he sees you.

We have a very strict rule at our house. DO NOT to scare our deaf dog on purpose. With as many rotten children I have had in my home, I knew we needed to establish this early. It is something I hold at a severe offense.

Even if you don't mean to do it, you will frighten this dog often. It still happens in our home about three times a week or so. I've included the sign for, "I'm sorry."

Give yourself some grace, and tell your puppy that you are sorry when it happens.

Lights
We talk a lot more about lights on page 51.

In the beginning, you need to be aware that lights are the same thing as a loud sound to your deaf dog. In deaf culture, flashing lights are used to get someone's attention. You see them used in alarms, doorbells, and phones.

So, think of it that way. A bright light is the same thing as a loud siren to your dog.

A lamp that suddenly comes on, thanks to Alexa, will make my dog jump every time. We always point to the light now as we ask her to turn it on. It signals River*, and she's prepared for it to happen. Then she won't bark at it. Lights turn my sweet dog into Cujo.

It is nothing unusual for a deaf dog to bark at the reflection of sunlight dancing across the ceiling of your living room. Our deaf dog barks at her own shadow! Literally! That's because it's an odd change of light. We see it as light, but it is so much more to a dog who depends so much on her other senses. We'll get more into why later in this book.

*Our deaf dog's name

> You are guilty of scaring the dog. Therefore, you are to: Tell the dog you are sorry, give her a treat, a scratch, and 100 push-ups, on your knuckles! All complaints have to be recorded in writing, with a minimum of ten vocabulary words.

Sorry

DEAF DOG

Food or Eat

Water

Did You Know?

Cats have up to 100 different vocalizations — dogs only have 10.

Feeding time

I have a dachshund, so believe me. Oscar knows when it's time to eat.

"All the time!" Oscar says!

When you first get your new dog, it's a good idea to lead them to their food bowl for the first few times. Sign "food" and then motion for your dog to follow you. This was how I taught River Roo her very first sign, and she learned it immediately.

Point to the water bowl and sign, "water."

As time goes on, you'll add more signs to your dog's vocabulary. I've included a dictionary in the back of this book.

There is also a chapter on the first signs that I recommend learning together with your dog.

Right by your side

Your new deaf dog may stick right to you at all times. Ours started this within a few days of living with us. I believe this is because I'm the one who signs the most to her. Well, that and I'm not a bad cook, either.

Even though they stick to you like glue most of the time, this dog shouldn't be allowed outside off of a leash unless you have a fenced-in yard to contain them. Over time, you may be able to trust them to stick right with you while you are outside.

Dog Noises
One of the questions we get the most is, "Does your deaf dog bark?"
I usually reply with, "Well, yeah. She's deaf, not mute!"

River Roo barks, just like a hearing dog does. She also moves her mouth and mumbles often. She has an odd, high-pitched tone that she will use to get our attention or tell our wiener dog that it's time to play.

Your deaf dog will make some of the oddest noises you have ever heard in your life. High-pitched whiney sounding barks and mumbling noises are the two I see the most with our deaf dog. I also think she believes she's speaking when she stands on her hind legs, pushing me into the counter, demanding more treats.

Not to worry. These odd noises are normal.

Of course, contact your vet if your dog does something that concerns you.

River's favorite time of day is when her Daddy comes home from work. He sits down and listens to her tell him all about her day.

And then that dang squirrel turned around and shook his butt at me! Can you believe that, Dad? That DANG SQUIRREL!

DEAF DOG

Then God said, "Let us make man in our image, after our likeness. And let them have dominion over the fish of the sea and over the birds of the heavens and over the livestock and over all the earth and over every creeping thing that creeps on the earth."

Genesis 1:26.

"And then he leaned over and scratched his dog." I whisper out of the side of my mouth.

It's a toxic Southern Trait that we all have to add our two cents worth in every conversation.

We even talk to bugs before we kill them. "You done messed up and flew into the wrong house today!"

Snoring
And while we're talking about noise, we should probably mention snoring. Good gravy, the snoring that comes from our deaf dog. Holy smokes. River has woken herself before!

Seriously, if anyone has tried Breathe Right Strips on a dog, let me know if it works. (Just kidding. Don't call PETA.)

Our family traditions for new pets
Our family has several unique traditions that I would like to share so that others may enjoy them, too. Adopting a pet is a big deal, so make a big deal of it.

Names
It usually takes our family about three or four days to decide what we would like to name our new pet.

Once the name has gets picked, we have a "Name Celebration Party." Nothing big, just some loud music, dancing and being silly. We've had a cake, new treats, and toys for all of our varmints in the past. It's just a way that we change up things from the everyday routine. But, I will confess there is another reason.

Owning a pet is a lifelong obligation you agree to when you bring a pet into your home. My husband and I concur on this point, *strongly*, and wanted to be sure to instill that into our son. You are adding a new family member—a responsibility.

We also give the new dog a blanket that belongs to only them. That makes it a bit easier when you put it in their crate and then point to it. I can also pull that blanket out if I'm sitting around watching television and want the dog to join me. I pat the blanket to invite the dog to wherever where I want them to be at the moment. That same blanket accompanies them to the vet, trips to the store, or when we go to see Grandma Woof Woof.

Our chihuahua loves his blanket so much that he will stand in front of the dryer and wait for it to get done when I finally can wash it.

Be patient with yourself and your new dog.
Not all dogs bond quickly with a new owner. Don't take it personally.

Dogs love having a routine.
Make a schedule, and stick to it. Plans provide comfort as your dog will begin to understand what to expect. Try to feed, walk them, and go to bed around the same time.

Also, keep in mind that **puppies will sleep a lot**. Just like human babies, they will need a lot of rest. And don't expect anyone to sleep through the night for the first few days. It just has never happened with us, and I've never heard anyone else having luck with that, either. In fact, Oscar will sometimes have a scary dream and need a piece of cheese at 3 a.m. And do you blame him? That 3 a.m. cheese just hits different.

Be consistent with the rules
I would recommend to have a family meeting and discuss these rules before even bringing your new pet home. If you already have pets, some restrictions may need to be added or revisited. Another thing you need to remind everyone, "This is a dog. Not a person. Do not think he can reason like a person. He will reason like a dog." As my grandfather used to say, "You can't put a human head on a dog." (Boy, that's Southern.)

Play with your dog
One of the best ways to bond with your dog is to play with them. Start with a simple game such as chase or fetch. Try rolling a ball away from them and see if they want to chase it. See more in the chapter on Training and Games.

Relax together
Hands down, hanging out together and watching TV after a long day is what our dogs must look forward to the most. Our wiener dog will tell us when he's had enough and demand us to join him in the living room at a particular time. He has us trained pretty well.

Exercise together
I enjoy a long walk and have found that my deaf dog loves it, too. You may try some other things: frisbee, fetch, swimming, jogging, tug of war, etc. Remember the leash and freshwater!

Our deaf dog wants to be part of what we're doing so much that she will often jump into the shower! You'll open your eyes, and she's standing right there.

If only she'd wash our back!

DEAF DOG

Practice some hand feeding
Offer the dog a treat from your outreached hand. This is an excellent technique to use if your new pet is shy or frightened. Be careful, though. If a dog is reacting aggressively, give them their space.

Be Patient, Consistent, and Positive
Remember my grandmother's advice, and smile at your new family member. While you're at it, smile at the rest of your family. As my son used to say when he was little, "It makes your face look better."

Work on some simple tricks
See the chapter on Training and Games.

Within the next three weeks, you will notice your dog will begin to settle into your routine. As your pet feels more comfortable, they will smile and wag their tail more often. Trainers believe that this is the point where the dog is beginning to think that this could be his forever home.

[handwritten: "fur-ever in River's case. Geez."]

Don't be surprised if your new dog tests the boundaries to see what is and is not allowed. Behavior issues do usually show up during this time.

Of course, talk to your vet about anything you find alarming.

After three months, your new pet should feel at home. Perhaps, you've noticed that the dog even has its routine. Or maybe, they have managed to train you into one!

[sticky note: You can do this.]

[sticky note: Your dog can do this.]

[sticky note: Patience is key.]

SIDE BARK

We camp a lot—both with and without our fur-babies. I'll admit that I've never left the house without a First Aid Kit for the "peoples," but I am surprised how many people travel without one for the canines of their party. It is just as important.

Here is a photo of our Chihuahua during one such camping trip. As you can see, Taco has just discovered that water is not something you can walk on top of.

Sorry to break it to you, Taco. You are not Jesus.

His Daddy has had to fish him out of the lake.

Later that evening, Taco fell off of the top of a picnic table onto his face. I still don't know why he was on top of the table, but it is what it is. Thankfully, he only suffered a busted lip and some wounded pride.

Taco isn't a fan of camping anymore.

But, Taco is thankful that his Mommy remembers always to bring a Pet First Aid Kit along. A little bit of doggie aspirin was a welcomed sight for this poor guy that night.

Pet First Aid Kits are available through Amazon. You may also want to talk to your local vet about medicines you should carry.

It's a good idea to have a lifevest for anyone on the water. Lifevests for dogs are available at pet stores and Amazon. Be sure to try it on them before setting out on the water. You'll want it tight enough that they won't slip out of it when their fur gets wet.

As I tell my son and his friends when they complain about having to wear a lifevest, "It only works if you are wearing it correctly."

Poor Taco thought he could walk on top of the water. Thankfully, his Daddy was close enough to grab him because he's not a strong swimmer. But, that face. That poor, pitiful puppy.

What we see.

What your dog sees.

Did you know?

Most scientists agree that dogs do not see in full color. Research shows that they see in shades of blue and yellow. Not black and white.

Dogs have only two rods in their eyes, whereas humans can have three or four!

However, dogs have a higher concentration of rod cells in their eyes, which enable them to see better in the dark and more aware of movement. Scientists believe deaf dogs have even more!

Another reason could also be because they rely on them more, and thus, they have a heightened sense of sight.

Most humans have three rods, which will allow them to see in shades of red, blue, yellow.

Tetrachormacy, or the presence of four cones in your eyes, is common among certain types of birds, reptiles, and fish. This extends the range of color vision into the ultraviolet scope. Doctors have even found some humans to have four cones, too! Tetrachromacy is more common in women than in men.

Some animals can see into the ultraviolent scope. However, it is something humans cannot do. The lens of a human's eye blocks the wavelength that contains it. So, your vision may be great, but because of your lens's limitations, you will not be able to use it to its full capacity.

Even though humans cannot see ultraviolet light directly because the lens of the eye blocks most light in that wavelength, get that? Your vision may be superior because of these extra cones, but because of your lens's limitations, you will not be able to use it to its full capacity.

DEAF DOG

Chapter 3: A crash course in Sign Language

Before you learn the first sign, it is essential to know that your expression on your face is the tone of your voice. That's not only for when signing to your dog, but when you are signing to anyone.

There is a vast difference between the following signs, even though they are the same word. See if you can figure it out.

Did you guess it correctly? I'm signing, "Hi." Can you see how much the tone of voice changes? How much my facial expressions changed?

My sister will tell you that I've greeted her with each one of these faces.

DEAF DOG

And guess what? "Hi," is your first sign that you will learn. And you probably already knew it. Trust me. There are a lot of words in ASL like that. *I have included a dictionary in the back of this book with signs we have found useful to teach River, our deaf dog.*

Keep in mind that this is their language. You are learning it and teaching it to your dog at the same time. Your dog is anxious to do things to get positive reinforcement. And, of course, treats go a long way, too. (In fact, River is asking me to insist that treats are the way to go.)

A dog's line of sight.

Just speak aloud to them while saying what you are signing, even if it's only one word. Usually, all it takes is a few words to get your message across. ASL is like that. Use the fewest words as possible to get your point across.

For example: You may say something like, "Do you want to play ball?" And actually only sign, "Ball." Or perhaps, "You play ball?"

Line of Sight
Keep in mind that you need to sign within the dog's line of sight. If your dog can't see your hands moving, she won't know what you are saying. Be sure to make eye contact with your dog.

Lights, tapping on the back, or stomping your foot are several ways to get your dog's attention. But, all of this is considered rude when trying to get a deaf person's attention.

Discretion should always be used with minimal movement. Waving your hand wildly in someone's face, jabbing someone in the shoulder, or stomping your foot can be seen as signs of aggression.

Flashing lights will annoy a deaf person or cause them to think there is an emergency.

My best advice is to gently tap someone on the shoulder or the back. Try to use a bent hand and make contact twice using your fingertips.

⚠ CAUTION

I don't understand. I read a book about sign language.

This book is about DOG Sign Language!

24   **DEAF DOG**

First Signs to Learn

I suggest you start with these signs first. Simply, speak naturally to your dog and sign them at the same time. The right expression on your face will most likely show up without you even trying. Remember, your facial expression is your tone of voice.

Dad - Father
What we use for my husband. The Dad.

Some names will not have signs for them, and you will have to invent one. This is called a "name sign" and is covered starting on page 35.

Mom - Mother
This is what we use for me. The Mom!

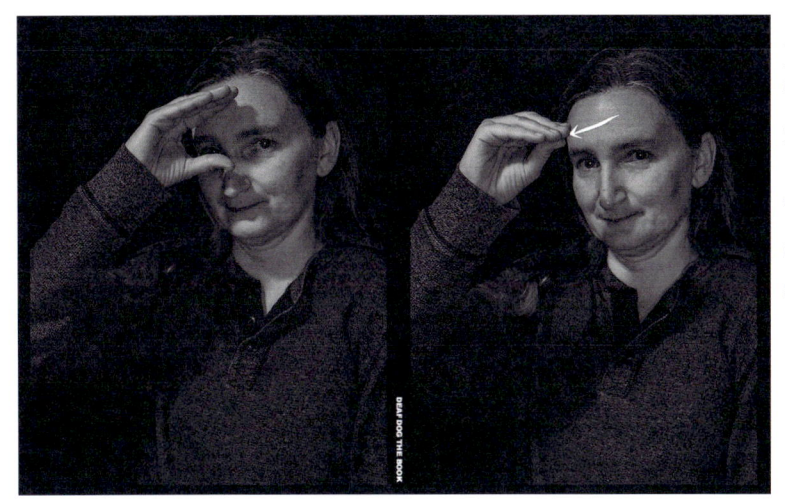

Boy
This is what we used for our son in the first few months.

The sign for brother is in this dictionary and is only one more step from this sign.

DEAF DOG

Girl
If you have a daughter or another female in the house, you may want to use this sign to keep it simple in the beginning.

Potty - Toilet
Let's face it; it's a vital sign. This is actually how you sign "toilet" in ASL. We use it to ask our deaf dog if she needs to go outside to do her business.

Water
Bounce three fingers against your chin and then point to the dogs' water bowl.

Does your dog make you roll your eyes with the things they do? Our wiener dog always seems to be in trouble about something. We have begun to call these, Oscar Moments. Tag us with your dog's, #OscarMoment

My quilt! Oscar Mayer Allen-Bender! What in the world-?

I'm sorry, Mom. I panicked.

26

DEAF DOG

Hello
Are you keeping up? You should have already seen this in this book. If you want to start counting, you'll see it once more.

Dog
This is a little different in ASL, but most deaf people would understand if you used this sign. For your dog, it is perfect.

No
And this photo maybe my newest meme. Now, if only my teenager would "friend me" on Facebook.

DEAF DOG

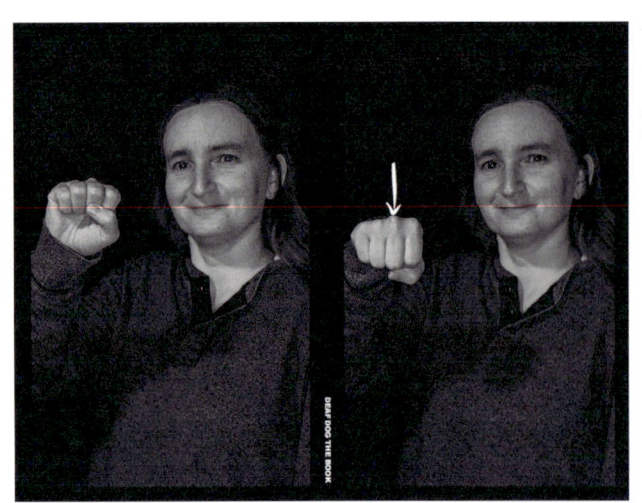

Yes
Shake your fist just as you would your head.

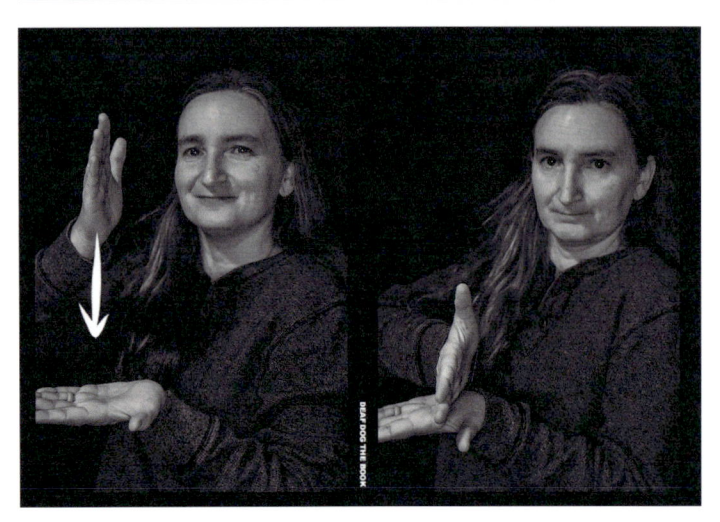

Stop
Remember your hand placement with this one. If you have to do it with one hand, use the top hand to convey your message.

Food
Have you got to eat, right?

Here's our River Roo looking for food.

28 DEAF DOG

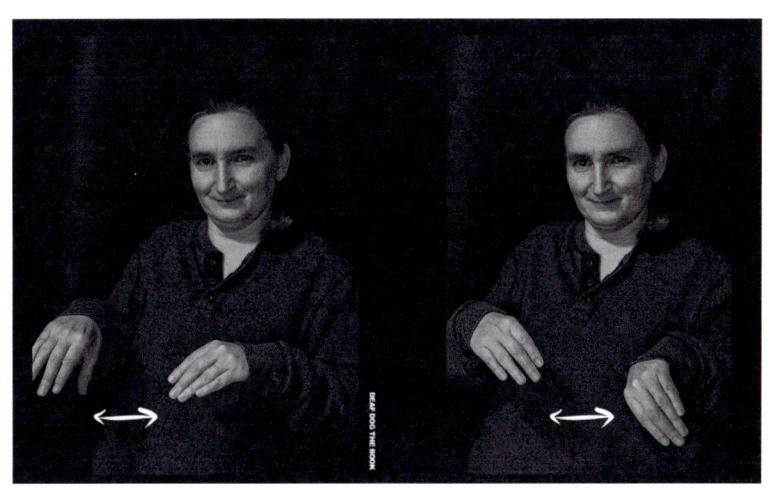

Treat

I just learned what this sign is. I'm including it because I wish I had started my dog with this, rather than only using food for her dog food and treats.

Good

Remember to praise your dog whenever she is doing something right! We are naturally programmed to "correct behavior," but also tell them when you see them doing what they are supposed to do.

Bad

Remember that you have to catch them doing something wrong rather than just telling them it is bad.

More information on that on page 38.

DEAF DOG

I can hear you now, "Alright, so how do we do this?"

Speak to your dog. Whenever you use those words, sign them to your dog.

> Some examples:
>
> When you go to the door to open it to allow the dog outside, sign "potty?"
>
> Point to the dog's water dish, swimming pool, puddle, or anything that is water and sign "water."
>
> When you feed the dog, a treat, sign "treat" or "food."
>
> When you are happy with them, sign "good."

Now, of course, this isn't going to be an instant thing. Your new dog is not only learning sign language but will probably also be feeling out the ropes of your home, deciding whether to trust you or not.

Remember to give yourself, and your dog, grace. You're going to make mistakes in signing, and your dog will misunderstand what you are sometimes saying. Believe me. It still happens here.

And it has hilarious consequences.

We have three dogs and a bearded dragon. That's too much to handle at once. We sometimes take *one* of our varmints to a pet store as a treat.

We have taken two at once, which resulted in a shoplifting incident by a wiener dog.

Oscar Mayer (our wiener dog) even caused a scene when he went to the pet store just on his own.

I had been feeding him some pumpkin treats, and apparently, they really move his bowels. Dude was so proud of his huge pile poo right there at the front door of the "posh" dog store.

Remember that scene in Jurassic Park when Jeff Goldbulm walks over to that massive pile of dinosaur poo and uttered those famous words, "Now, that is one big pile of #$%@."? Yeah, that was what the store employee said, too.

I was all like, "Oscar Mayer. Stop poo'ing. Are you kidding me? Oh my gosh, I'm so sorry. Oh my, OSCAR! Are you serious? Why are you going do-do in the middle of the store? Oz. Stop that! Really, nasty dog! What did you eat? The actual heck, OZ! Stop that! Oh, Lord, help me with this dog. Oscar! Bad dog. With that pooping! You're going to throw your back out with that stra- OZ! Dang it, dog, are you even listening to me? I'm so sorry. He never does this at home. Do you hear me, man!? Why are you doing this here! You were just outside! Are you still pooping? You've got to be kidding. OSCAR! Oh, my stars!...."

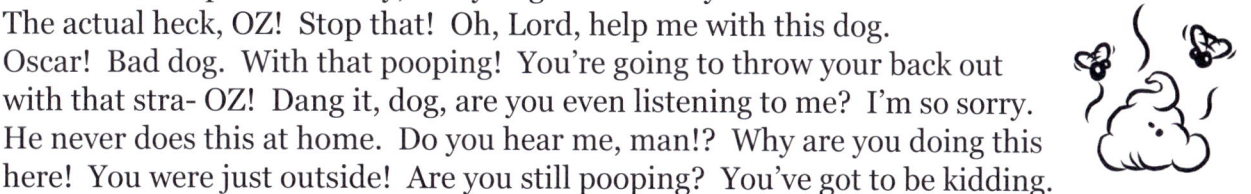

Seriously, we haven't been back to that pet store again.

The employee told us they were used to it, but I just couldn't.

This wiener dog. Ugh! He's so extra—all the time. Seriously, if I'm telling someone to stop doing something in this house, it's usually him. I hear it's a Doxie trait.

When we took River Roo to the pet store for the first time, I remember she was so scared of the automatic doors sliding in front of her. My husband had to pick her up and carry her into the store. She got to pick a toy and treats for her and the other monsters waiting back home. When people saw she had "Deaf Dog" written on her collar, they all stopped to pet her. She ate it up and fell utterly in love with going for a ride to the pet store.

This wasn't something we had even thought about when my husband took her to a home improvement warehouse one weekend.

"Did you put the poop story in here? How embarrassing!"

DEAF DOG

River stood in the shopping cart, and James held onto the loose leash as he pushed her into the store. As soon as she saw that same sort of sliding doors, her face must have lit up like Christmas. She dove out of that shopping cart and ran all over the place!

I'm sure my poor husband looked like a terrible dog owner because he didn't even bother to scream for her.

Why should he?

She can't hear him!

Poor guy found one of the employees there and told them that his dog was loose in the store.

"She's friendly, but she's deaf."

The employee immediately helped. Getting on his walkie-talkie, he informed the other store associates what was going on.

Within seconds, they heard the great news that River was safe with an employee. When James made it over there to them, she licked the man's face and got all the "scratchies."

"She's so friendly!" He smiled. All was well.

James wanted to make sure that River understood this was not appropriate behavior.

After getting her attention, he signed. "No."

She lowered her ears sadly and gave him her best puppy dog eyes.

James continued, "Good girl."

She smiled and wagged her tail as if to say, "That's right. I'm a good girl."

Seeing she wasn't understanding,

James tried again. "No."

She looked confused and tilted her head.

(signed) "Good girl."
She jumped around and barked happily. "That's right. I'm a good girl! Yeah!"

In this case, I don't think she would have understood what he was trying to say. She still hadn't realized she wasn't in the pet store.

And I've screwed up, too. More than once. Recently. But hey, it had been a while.

Whenever I get chicken from a specific restaurant, I bring home nuggets for the dogs. The sign I've always used for this is simply "chicken."

I was out running errands one day and picked up some toys for the varmints. One stuffed toy was a chicken that rattled like it has a plastic bottle inside.

I handed it to her and signed, "Chicken."

She immediately dropped it and began to drool.

I looked at her in surprise. "Woman, why are you looking at me like a steak dinner?"

She jumped up on me and barked. "Where is the chicken?"

"Chill out. What's your problem?"

Then I realized what I was signing.

So, now the toy is called "turkey." And delicious nuggets can remain, "chicken."

"Mom brought home some chicken! Stop being a Wiener and get up your tail up here."

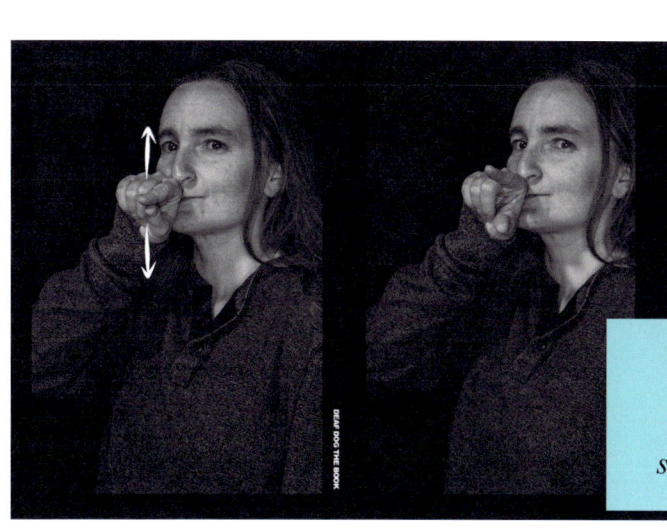

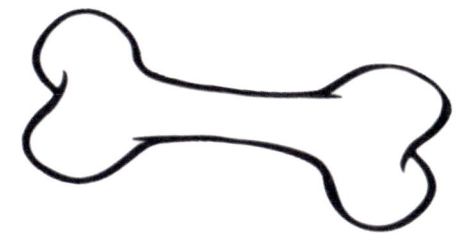

Sign for chicken or bird (My sister eats so much chicken that her name sign looks similar to this.)

DEAF DOG 33

Applause and Cheering

When I was house training Oscar, I never thought he would get the whole "pooping outside" thing.

Dachshunds are notoriously stubborn, and Oscar was no different. I even thought about giving up and looking at doggie diapers. Did you know that their model on their packaging is a Dachshund? That was not a good sign.

I can remember calling my mother-in-law and complaining.

"This dog is going to the death of me. If I do die, promise to come to my funeral and do not let anyone mention house training."

She may have accused me of being dramatic.

I remember her telling me that he was looking for positive reinforcement. In some ways, puppies are just like a child.

That makes sense. I mean, if my dog goes outside and pees in the yard, and I cheer like I've won the lottery, they are going to want to see their owner that happy again, right?

It does make me wonder if they actually worry about our state of mental well being and just take pity on us. Imagine the dog squatting and straining, only to look up and see their owners cheering and carrying on like an idiot.

Your deaf dog can't hear clapping but can see your hands when you wave them next to your head. And that's what is used for applause in American Sign Language.

How did I house train our deaf dog then? Whenever she went outside and "did her business," she would look back to me and see me applauding for her, in her language.

What applause looks like. Use this in place of clapping. I also have seen it used for the words, "Awesome!", "Great!"

River wants me to add that she also gets a treat as soon as we return to the house.

Chapter 4: Name Signs

A name sign is a sign for someone's name. Yeah, it sounds obvious enough, but you would be surprised how many times I've been asked.

American Sign Language doesn't have a way to sign every word, or name, in English.

For example: Sharon.

(Sharon is our next-door neighbor and River Roo's Auntie.)
You can either spell Sharon....

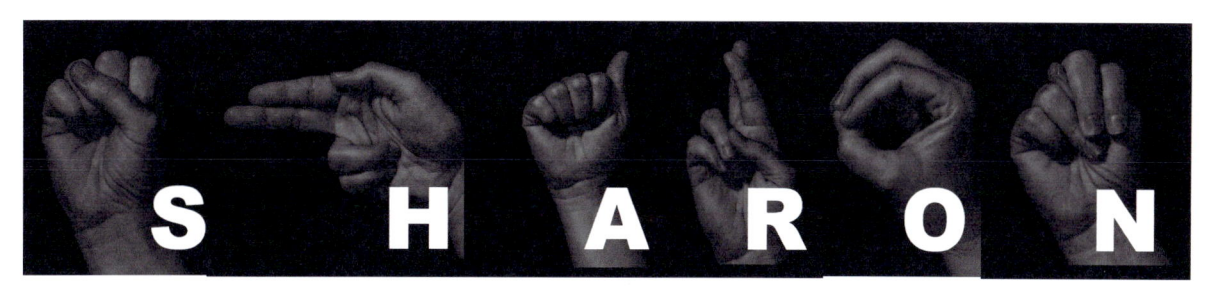

S H A R O N

Man, that's a lot of work. Imagine signing that every time you use Sharon's name.

Well, lucky for you, I'm going to explain to you how to make a name sign, so you don't have to do this. Trust me, and it's going to be a lot easier.

REAL-WORLD SIGNING:
Because almost everyone will have to have a name sign created for them, there is a pattern for introducing yourself when you first meet someone who is deaf.
You would sign:
"Hi. My name is C-H-R-I-S-T-I."
Then, sign your name sign.
Of course, you do not have to follow this pattern with your dog. Please do with "a people."

DEAF DOG 35

Our friend, Sharon, is a police officer. So, let's start with the sign for the police.

Just imagine a badge there on her uniform. Make the sign for "C" and place it on your chest, as shown.

Police

Sharon's name begins with an "S." So, the most straight forward name sign we can make will be to use an "S" and put it to our chest like we would if we were signing, "police."

Isn't that easier than signing out her full name?

Sharon's name sign

Another example
Our groomer's name is Amy.

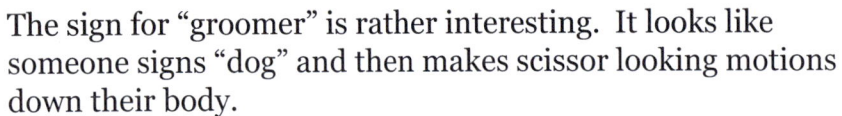

A M Y

Bath

The sign for "groomer" is rather interesting. It looks like someone signs "dog" and then makes scissor looking motions down their body.

I opted not to use that sign because it was a bit aggressive looking, and it scared River the first time she saw it.

Instead, I use something similar to the sign for "bath."

Name sign we use for Amy.

36 **DEAF DOG**

Line of Sight

Remember to keep in mind the angle that your dog sees your signs.

When we were picking Taco and Oscar's name signs, we ran into a problem because of this. From the bottom, looking up, they all appear that we are signing the same word. Look at the images below These are three different signs. But, from your dog's point of view, they appear to be the same three!

These are three different signs. (front the left) stop, taco, hot dog.

In the beginning, I only recommend making signs for people who live in your home.

When your dog gets those, introduce people who visit often.

I encourage you to add new names to your dog's vocabulary often. Always have them learning something new. It helps you both!

Avoid changing name signs whenever possible. I would recommend just adding something to it. That is what I'd found to be easier to train to my deaf dog.

Our son is a literal sort of person and didn't want a name sign. Instead, he opted just to be called "brother." He thought it would be easier to sign, and he didn't run the risk of accidentally signing something offensive.

Name signs are traditionally only given to a hearing person by a deaf person.

Here's a fun thing to ask yourself. What sign to you think your dog would pick for you? For themselves?

Want to double-check the name sign you have picked is not something offensive? No problem. Tag us using #namesignhelp

DEAF DOG

Chapter 5
Dog Psychology and Training

It is important to remember that no matter how much we think of them as little furry people, your dog is a dog! Your dog will do things we think are just crazy for people, but they are a dog! That's just normal behavior for them.

I'll never understand why they believe that rolling in something that would gag the Roto-Rooter man is the best thing in the world.

A muddy backyard? Oh gosh.

And did mention my dog with a snow-white coat of fur? (We find out why on page 61.)

I had let her outside to run around while I cleaned our pool. I didn't think ahead to the fact that water would spill over to the Georgia Red Clay. And by the time I found her, oh wow. She had the best time!

I decided that it didn't make much sense to fuss at her about it. It was my fault. I mean, who wouldn't have done that?

I mean, what DOG wouldn't have done that?

Go ahead, ask yours and see what they say.

A muddy River.

"Aww. Mom! A bath? Really?"

DEAF DOG

But, what if it was something that you wanted them never to do again. Some behavior you didn't want them to repeat, like rolling in horse poop. (It has happened here.)

Keep in mind that the dog has limited reasoning abilities. If you tell them not to do something that they haven't done in the previous ten seconds….it's just a waste of time.

I've read a lot about this because I think it may affect teenage boys, too. They simply can't remember what they were doing.

Or, the language barrier between humans and dogs is just so much that we can't make them understand that we're not angry at something they have done.

Hang on, "Oscar! You can wear the jacket, but don't eat it."

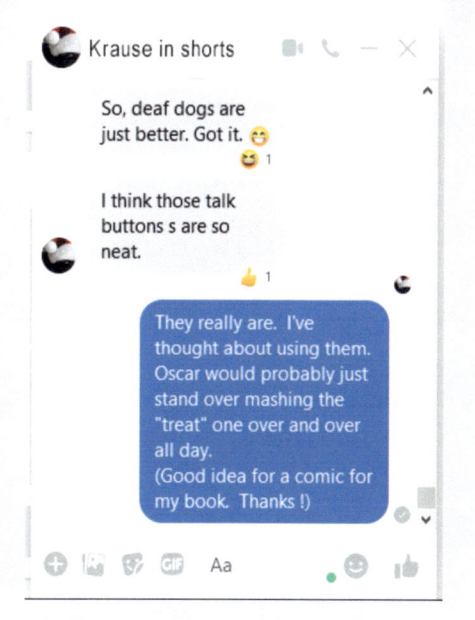

Meanwhile, at home (aka, the trench)

When I was editing the text of this particular chapter, I took a break and walked into the kitchen to fix myself a glass of tea. This is how I found Miss River Roo.

"What in the world?" I exclaimed, but of course, she didn't hear me.

At first glance, the rotten dog is lying on top of the kitchen table.
"What the what? That's totally against the rules! No!

When we look closer, we'll see that River is lying up there so she can see the squirrels out of the window.

As a pet psychologist, it's just part of me to investigate not only the "what"...but find the reason "why" of the behavior, too. She wants to lay down and be comfortable when she's looking outside. Wouldn't we all?

I know I would.

I move a couple of my dining room chairs around to make a bench that will put her eye-level with the window. I even cushion it for her with a blanket.

She watches as I do this and begins to wag her tail.

As soon as it's finished, she jumps off of the table and onto my makeshift bench.

Sometimes in life, it pays to simply slow down and see what is really going on.

40   DEAF DOG

Imagine if we could speak the same language. Just briefly. How nice would that be?

On any given day...

- "Ah-rooooo!!!!"
- "Oscar-Mayer Allen-Bender!"
- "Ruh-row."
- "Could you **not** suddenly jump up and howl at the dang Amazon man? I had to peel myself off the ceiling again!"
- "I'm sorry."
- "Next time, could you please just....warm up with an easy, light bark? Like...an Eagle's song bark?"
- "'Hotel California-'"
- "I'm thinking, 'Peaceful, Easy, Feeling.'"
- "I get 'cha!"

C. Bender

But, alas, we live in the real world. Instead, it should go something like this.

(signed), *"River! Do not go into the pasture. You will get hurt."*

River looks over at the horses running in the pasture. Then she looks back at me and whines. I'm sure she's saying, "But, Mom! Those huge dogs!"

(signed) *"I mean it. NO! You want a treat, don't you? Want to go back to the house?"*

"Yay! House!" River smiles and begins to run towards the house.

Sometimes, redirection works like in this example. And this Momma is always for the easy option.

DEAF DOG

An electronic collar

I hate this. Hate this. HATE THIS..... but my husband and I spoke to a friend of ours who used to have a K9. He recommended that we get a shock collar for our deaf dog.

James bought one, and I told him that we were not using that on her under any circumstances. I tucked it away in the house.

Then, some many months later, we pulled it out during a dare with a friend of ours. This grown man lost the bet and had to wear it while he was shocked once at 25% by one of the guys.

(I've been corrected. It was at 100%. Twice. And while he was sitting in an aluminum chair!)

Yeah, you've had an insight into our crazy cook-outs with friends. I believe that our teenage son could possibly be the most mature out of all of us.

After seeing that our friend lived through it and honestly said it didn't hurt, I had a different opinion. But, I still wasn't prepared for the phone call I got a few weeks later from my son.

"Mom. You need to get home right now."

"Why? What's wrong?"

"Dad has that shock collar on River."

"Sir? Are you calling to tell on your father?"

And indeed, he was calling to do just that.

I reassured him that his Dad knew what he was doing, and I'd look into it when I got home.

I remember ending the call and grumbling under my breath, "James, you better know what you are doing or......" grumble, grumble.

Unsupervised Man.

See that white dot right there? That's our deaf dog. Thanks to the vibration signal on an electronic collar, we can call her back when we think she's gone too far while giving her the freedom to play, run around, and explore.

DEAF DOG

After I found out the entire situation, I can't say I approved entirely of it. My husband told me he didn't have the collar over 50% of its shocking capability. He had even tried it on himself before he had done it to her.

"It feels a bit like those lighters that shock you. Remember the sort that you used to be able to get when you were a kid?"

"What? No-"

"Yeah. It was a prank thing. Gas stations sold them."

River Roo!
Master of Disguise!

"Wow." I teased. "The things you miss out on living in a small town."

"It didn't hurt her. And I only had to shock her twice. Once when she under the fence of the pasture, and another time she had gotten into it. The rest of the time, I have been using the vibration button on it-"

"Hang on? What?"

"Yeah. You press this button, and her collar will vibrate. She knows it means, "Come back."

River was running all over the place with Oscar in the field about 150 feet from where we were standing. Way further than she had ever been in our yard without a leash. She looked like she was having the time of her life.

If you use an electronic collar, remove it before your dog gets in or around water. This may not even be a big deal at all, but I always insist on doing it.

DEAF DOG

He pressed the button, and I watched as our deaf dog lifted her head. Just as if he had called her name. James motioned for her just as he said, "Come on! Bring her up here, Ozzy. Mom is home!"

River and Oscar ran right up to us.

How did he do this? He said it was so simple. He turned on the collar and set it to vibrate. He walked away from the dog, turned, and pressed the button while motioning for her to come to him. All of this happened while he was standing in the driveway.

"Whenever she came to me, I told her she was a 'good girl' and scratched her face. Then I would let her go again. She ran around the yard, explored places she's probably never been because of the limitations of a leash, and stayed right with Oscar. Every so often, I'd return to the driveway and press the button to make her collar vibrate. She always ran directly back, and of course, received praise each time."

Vibration control – So, after writing all of that about how I was not too fond of the entire idea of using a shock collar, I'm going to tell you to get one. This dog can't hear you call her! If she's not going to be inside the safety of a fence, she needs to have it on.

As our friend told us, "It's like having her on a loose leash. When you press that button to vibrate it, it's just like taking that leash and giving it a gentle tug to get her attention."

Some dogs will carry around a particular plush doll loosely in their mouths. They will snuggle with it when they sleep or insist it comes along with them when they go someplace.

This behavior is often seen in dogs taken from their mothers and littermates before they were entirely weaned.

Puppy mill survivors and those orphaned as puppies often act out nursing and littermate behaviors on their soft toys. Mothers who lost their pups or experienced false pregnancies may also treat a plushy as their lost pup.

These activities are only problematic if they become obsessive, lead to aggression, or pose a risk of swallowing part of the toy.

Training Games

For a dog that doesn't rely on her hearing, you have to train and play a bit differently. As a homeschool Mom, I've learned that it's effortless to combine play into learning over the years. And I'm going to explain how to do just that with your dog. It's just like sneaking those vegetables your kids won't eat into something they will.

Let me state as plain as I can right here. I am NOT a pet trainer. The following are just the steps that I did to train my deaf dog. I believe that anyone can train any dog as long as they are consistent, patient, and use a lot of love. And treats, of course!

Remember to smile every time you look into your dog's face. Your expression is your tone of voice to your dog. Keep that in mind when you are training.

The first game, maybe the most important one that you'll ever use to train your dog. I call it, "Look at me."

A deaf dog cannot see you sign (or talk) to them if they aren't looking at you.

Look at Me

Step 1: Wave to your dog to get their attention.
Step 2: When they look at you, sign their name, and smile. Then wait a bit. Count to five without taking your eyes off of your dog. You can even count aloud so they can see your lips move. My son also has counted on his fingers so she can see the progression. I think that's wise and recommend you do that.
Step 3: If they continue to look at you after the five seconds, give them a treat.
Repeat this game often.

Don't get discouraged if this is difficult to master. It's one of the hardest things that I have trained River to do. And honestly, if she's not interested in what I have to say, she still won't do it.

Holding treats in your hands defiantly helps!

DEAF DOG

Fetch - Nothing beats this old classic.
Use the sign for "Ball" when it's fetch playing time!

Step 1: I took River Roo into our backyard and showed her a tennis ball. When she attempted to get it from me, I rolled it away from us.
(That's right. Please don't throw it at first. It can startle your dog.)
Step 2: She chased it and picked it up in her mouth.
Step 3: I motioned for her to come to me, and I traded the toy for a small treat. Don't worry if this takes many attempts to get your dog to bring it back to you. Remain calm and patient. This is meant to be fun for both of you.
Step 4: Repeat.

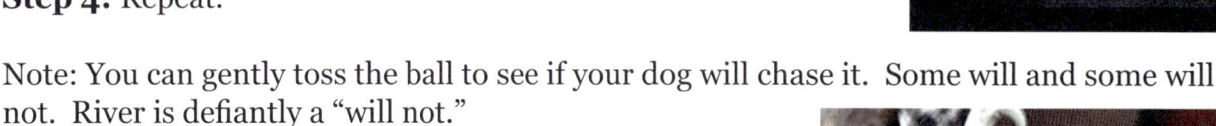

Note: You can gently toss the ball to see if your dog will chase it. Some will and some will not. River is defiantly a "will not."

Try a frisbee instead of a ball, too!

Your dog may also enjoy a balled up sock! Give it a try!

One Christmas, River Roo received a box full of tennis balls from Santa

The internet is full of fun things you can teach your dog to do. When training your deaf dog, be sure to use the same signs for the action to eliminate confusion. It is also extremely important to remember that your facial expression is your tone of voice. Remember to smile and keep a playful, upbeat attitude!

Sit
Step 1: Wait until your dog sits down on its own.
Step 2: Smile and give a treat as you sign, "Sit."
Step 3: Repeat
Step 4: Sign "Sit"
Step 5: When the dog sits, give them a treat and smile!

Lay down

Step 1: Wait until your dog lays down. It will sometimes happen right after they sit.
Step 2: When the dog lays down, smile and sign "lay down." Also, give a treat.
Step 3: Repeat.
Step 4: Sign "Lay down"
Step 5: When the dog lays down, give them a treat and smile!

The best place to teach this is at night time, as they are going to bed. I may sign it in my sleep most nights.

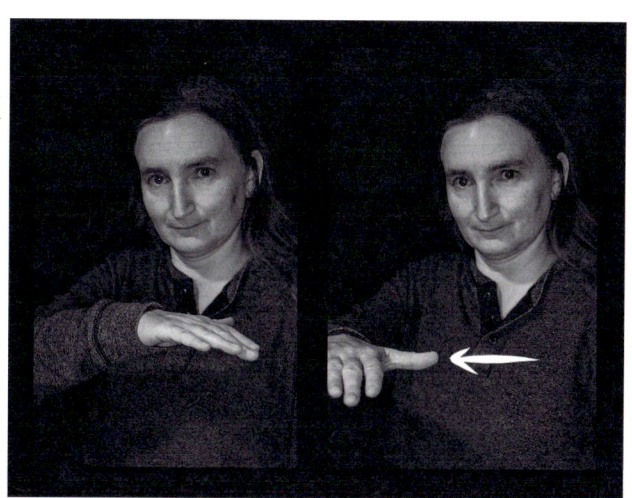

Stay

Step 1: Ask your dog to sit. Smile and give them a treat when they do.
Step 2: Sign "Stay" and wait five seconds. Counting aloud may help because your dog can see your lips move. You can also count using your fingers so that your dog will be able to see the progression.
Step 3: Walk a few steps back as you are counting. Remember to keep eye contact with your dog.
Step 4: Smile and wave your dog to come to you.
Step 5: When they do, give them lots of praise. Smile and give them a treat.

When using sign language, you want to get your point across using the least amount of signs possible. Also, in ASL, the adjective goes behind the noun that it is describing. Since you are using this with your dog, it's really not terribly important. But it is something you need to be aware of if you decide to expand your study of ASL after reading this book.

DEAF DOG

Games that Train!
One thing I've learned over the years is that if you make a game out of a chore, children will learn it so much faster. Well, I think Mary Poppins may have actually said that first. But, hey. It works! Ole girl is onto something!

Dogs are no different in this aspect. In fact, this is the only way to get that dang Dachshund of ours to do anything I ask him.

Sigh. That dog.

Where are you?
Sometimes, I'll walk into a room to discover River and Oscar sitting in the window seat looking out the window. I'll look around as if I'm unable to see them and sign, "Where are River and Oscar?" Or, more literally, I sign, "Where Oscar River?"

Both of them will bark as if to say, "We are here, Mom!"

I'm sure they think I'm nearly blind, or crazy, or both! But, let's look at what this is reinforcing. First, the "Look at me" command. You can sign all you want to your deaf dog, but if she's not looking at you, there's no point. Also, what if your dog was someplace where they could clearly see you, but you were unable to see them? Wouldn't you want them "trained" to answer when you called them?

The "Where Are You" Game is also a great way to teach your dog(s) more vocabulary in sign language. Sign, "Where ball?" or "Where Daddy?" and then help your dog find whatever you have asked them. When you find the person or object, cheer and praise the dog. They will grow to understand this the more you do it.

Some examples:
See the dictionary for more vocabulary words!

Where doll?   *Where camper?*
Where water?   *Where home?*
Where cat crazy?   *Where brother your?*
Where steak?   *Where squirrel?**

* Our family's favorite game.

Psychologists say that human children need to hear something repeated seven times before they remember it. I'm going to climb out on a limb and say that dogs will need more examples than that. Maybe, fourteen times? Unless they are a Dachshund like mine, in that case, forget it—best of luck to you on that.

Hide the Ball

Our teenager discovered that our tennis ball junkie likes having a ball put into an old sock. Well, perhaps "likes" isn't the right word. Rather, a tennis ball shoved into a sock will keep her busy for a while. We have also put treats, bones, or deer antlers in the sock. River will grab the sock in her mouth and shake it violently.

I recommend that you only use socks you no longer want to keep. Also, tie one end of the sock to keep the tennis ball from flying out and smacking someone in the head.

Sound like something she's going to have to use some higher reasoning skills to sort out? Well, you're right. This type of toy is often referred to as a Puzzle Toy. There are several that you can purchase.

Let's play!

We ordered our deaf dog a plush puzzle toy with these cute, tiny, squeaky squirrels that she has to pull out of the tree log. It's adorable, but I'll warn you. Those dang squirrels are all over our house now!

Sniffle Mat

Another toy that the entire pack enjoys is a sniffle mat. I had never heard of this before I started writing this book, but they are now one of River's favorite things. It reminds me of those playmats you put your baby on when it's tummy time. This mat has little strips of cloth used to hide treats. I usually break the treats apart before hiding them.

Using a sniffle mat with their food will also slow down a quick eater.

I'll have to say that the sniffle mat will wear your dog straight out. After a demanding search for their favorite treats, my entire pack will lay down and sleep for hours. Be sure that it's machine washable. It does get gross with dog snot pretty quickly.

Taco looks for a treat trapped in the sniffle mat.

Do you have a game you like to play with your dog? Share it with us #doggames

DEAF DOG

Under the Cup
This game is one that my son often plays with our pack. He will hide a treat under a cup and then move them around really fast in front of River. She can always keep up with him, and it's so cute to see her use her cold nose to pick out where the treat is.

Another variation of this game uses the same principle. My son will hide a piece of a treat under a cup and walk away. I've seen twenty red cups spread all over the house at once. The dogs love this game and will rush to find those cups. Oscar will knock them over with his big, ole nose while River uses her hand to swat it over. Our chihuahua finds this sort of thing extraordinarily foolish and will sit and watch the other two.

There are other puzzle toys that you can make using things you probably already have around your house.
Just use your imagination. River will pull these baby socks off of the stuffed animal.

And of course, always supervise your dog while playing.

That is the stupidest display of canine behavior that I've ever seen. Just give me the dang treat.

50 DEAF DOG

Chapter 6

Lights are LOUD!

One of the most surprising things to discover was our deaf dog's reaction to any changes in light, whether it was a shadow or a reflection.

I took some junk food out of our air fryer one day when suddenly River went utterly crazy! She was growling, snarling, with her hair standing up all over her neck and back.

I'm not going to lie. My first thought was, "Well, this is how it all ends—attacked by a chicken addict who was offended to the inferior, store brand nugget."

I sat the fryer tray on the cabinet, and she stopped barking.

I picked it back up, and she began to bark at the ceiling and growl again. By this time, she also had the other dogs talking trash too.

I looked up and spotted what had alarmed her. The light was bouncing against the metal of the tray, sending a reflection to the ceiling. To test my theory, I moved around the tray. River followed the light and became more aggressive with her warning bark.

Why had I never thought about this? Well, how often do you think about it? Let's take a moment to do just that.

How do people who are deaf:

- know when to answer their phone?
- wake get up at a specific time in the morning?
- know that someone is at the door?

DEAF DOG

When I was in college, I visited the dorms at the Georgia School for the Deaf. Several friends of mine lived there. It was there where I got this answer to this question. And the short answer is **light**.

Alarm clocks, doorbells, and even their phones alert them using a flashing light. Because the deaf depend so much more on their sense of sight, this works beautifully.

My friend signed to me. "Think of it as if a light is a thunderous noise to someone who is deaf."

So, let's go back to us standing in the kitchen with River now foaming at the mouth like a mad dog, ready to lose her mind entirely at a reflection.

I put the tray back into the air fryer, which stopped the light that had offended River so much.

I signed "light" to her and then gave her a reassuring scratch.

Have you heard the expression that someone is scared of their own shadow?
That's our River.

As soon as I remembered this little fact about deaf culture, I became very conscious of any light changes around our home. This information brought my attention to the strangest things that I hadn't realized were frightening our deaf dog.

River is scared of anything on television with bright, sudden lights. Such as the sort that appears as bright flashes of lasers on the screen.

I also realized that since my husband had changed his bedside light, River had completely stopped sleeping on that side of the bed. She was now sleeping under the covers right up next to me. Was it the light that had frightened her?

52   DEAF DOG

There are ways that you can use light to your and your dog's advantage. Very often, I will use my cell phone to get River's attention. I turn on the screen and turn the phone towards her. It will remain lit for a few seconds, which is just long enough to get her attention most of the time. I have found this works with her, even in the daylight, if she's close enough to me. We will also use the flashlight on our phones, turn it away from us and wave it over our heads. That's very useful.

Like many people, we have Alexa in our home. My husband has programmed this "other woman" to control most of the lights in our home. And, yep. You probably guessed it. River hates it.

Wave your phone around to get your dog's attention in the dark.

You don't even have to think about this too long to realize why my deaf dog hated these lights. At least when we turn on a traditional "wall-switch" light, River gets the signal that a light is about to come on. Even if it's just a few seconds, she has a bit of preparedness for it.

And it makes sense if you think of the light here as something very loud. So, let us consider this....What if every night, you walked into a room and a thunderous rock song played? As long as you were expecting it, it doesn't cause any fright. Maybe that's the same situation with the deaf dog and the bedroom light.

But, what happens when we remove the "wall-switch"? We eliminate the preparedness of the activity. And thus, the loud rock song blares us completely out of the room and sends us into a panic.

You can do simple things to signal to your dog that a light is about to turn on, tapping the light switch, creating a sign, or maybe something even more straightforward.

My son noticed that I pointed to the ceiling as I spoke to Alexa to turn it on the light.

"What are you doing?"

"I point at the light so River knows it's about to come on."

He exclaims. "We've come full circle."

Sunlight that dances on the ceiling during the afternoon is a very frightening thing to most deaf dogs.

DEAF DOG 53

Chapter 7

When deaf dogs react to sound

I can see you now. "Hang on. React to a sound? This dog can't hear!"

I know. It's crazy. The first time my teenage son saw this happen, he became convinced that River was recovering from something that had caused her to go deaf and was improving. I'm not saying that can't happen, but I knew it wasn't the case with us.

The entire event happened when I was playing the drums. River loves music and will lie down in front of my amp. I play an electric set, so that's where all the sound comes out. When I stop playing, River will turn and complain.

My son noticed her behavior, "Look, Mom! She can hear that!"

"No, honey. She can feel it."

I had him put earplugs in and lay on the floor next to River so he could feel the music, too.

My son was impressed but then realized he had done a bad thing. A very terrible thing indeed. He had given this homeschool Mom an idea for a unit study. A unit study is when you study one subject in great depth. Lessons from a unit study will spill over into courscs in every subject a homeschool child is studying.

Or, as my teenager puts it, "When Mom decides to torment her poor, helpless students."

Note from Mom's student: It is! Send Help!

My deaf dog is my drumming coach.

River Roo is working on her album pose.

54   **DEAF DOG**

Whatever, kid. Taco has never complained. And let's face it, he's leading in the Student of the Month awards at the moment. We won't even talk about how unlikely it will ever be that Oscar will ever get one unless he steals it.

What is sound?
Sound is Energy.

"Energy? What?"

Sit back and let his homeschooling Momma impress you.

Sound is energy that travels in waves. These waves are measured in frequency and amplitude. The energy in a sound wave is measured in decibels. So, thus decibels is how we describe how loud something is.

As hearing people, our ears are sensitive to the wide range from quiet to loud that we can perceive.

This is often shown as a decibel scale.

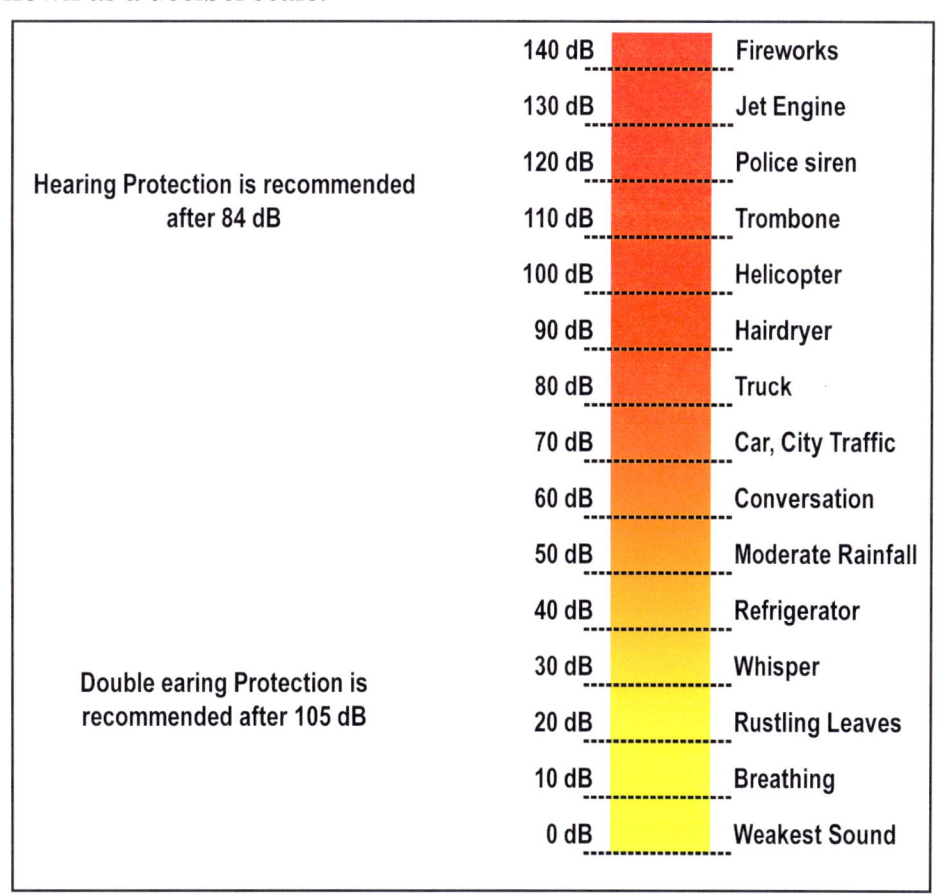

Hearing Protection is recommended after 84 dB

Double earing Protection is recommended after 105 dB

dB	Source
140 dB	Fireworks
130 dB	Jet Engine
120 dB	Police siren
110 dB	Trombone
100 dB	Helicopter
90 dB	Hairdryer
80 dB	Truck
70 dB	Car, City Traffic
60 dB	Conversation
50 dB	Moderate Rainfall
40 dB	Refrigerator
30 dB	Whisper
20 dB	Rustling Leaves
10 dB	Breathing
0 dB	Weakest Sound

DEAF DOG

Alright, that's just measuring how loud things are. We're talking about the sound moving.

To prove this theory, I think it would be best to look at the simple opera singer vs. glass experiment.

Everything, including a piece of glass, has a point where it will break when it is disturbed by an outside stimulus. This is called a **natural resonant frequency.**

In the case of glass, the sound wave travels through it, causing it to vibrate. Any sound waves can, and will, produce sympathetic vibrations on materials close to them. This is the principle that makes telephones and radars work. As the volume increases, it displaces air molecules. The sound will pass from molecule to molecule until it hits the glass.

But, we're talking about breaking the glass. To do that, you would need to find not only the right frequency but also amplitude that is high enough to exceed the strength of the glass to resist those vibrations.

Simply put, when the sound becomes too loud for the glass to vibrate, it causes the glass to shatter.

> Oh my dog! Kidney Stones!
>
> Mom said she'd rather have children three at a time than ever to have one of those again.
>
> C. Bender

If you suffer from kidney stones, you are already familiar with this process. Doctors use **Extracorporeal Shock Wave Lithotripsy (or ESWL)** to break up kidney stones. They don't spend time searching for the perfect resonant frequency, though. They blast the stone with lots of sound energy. The sound energy causes kidney stones to break up, making them easier to pass.

After Beethoven went deaf, he found he could attach a metal rod to this piano and bite down on it while he played. This enabled him to hear through vibrations in his jawbone. The process is called bone conduction.

Did you know?

Dogs of all breeds can suffer from chapped pads on their feet?

At the beginning of the spring, we opened our pool and bought this speedboat for our dogs to chase around until it got warm enough for them to go swimming.

My lips were chapped, but I didn't even think that my dogs' pads were also chapped.

After about ten minutes of playing on the pool deck, we spotted blood. Both River and Oscar had rubbed most of the pads off their feet!

The vet gave them both antibiotics, kept their feet wrapped, and kept them still for about a week. It was painful, but both of them made a full recovery.

To prevent this, get a lotion that is specially made for your dogs' feet. When your lips are chapped or the weather changes, check your dogs' feet, too. Apply as directed.

Also, never allow your pets to walk on hot asphalt or concrete to prevent the pads of their feet from being burnt.

Chapter 8: Is your dog deaf?

How can you tell if your dog is deaf?
There are some signs that you can keep an eye out for in an old dog and a brand new puppy. Keep in mind, though, that all puppies of all breeds are born deaf. Their ear canals are closed until they are around 10-14 days old.

Once your puppy is over 14 days old, you may ask yourself, "Is my puppy deaf or just stubborn?"

Some things to look out for:
Does the puppy bite their littermates harder than the other ones?

If the puppy can't hear their littermates complaints, they will continue to play harder. This is also something you need to keep in mind as your dog ages. They can't hear when their playmates growl or complain that they are getting too rough. You will need to step in and remind your deaf dog to be careful.

If they don't hear the food bowl, they will not show up to eat. *Do you have to show the dog their food?*

Do their ears move in response to sounds happening around them? If not, they may not be hearing them.

Is your dog easily startled? Did she hear you walk up behind her?

DEAF DOG

Does your dog greet you at the door when you come home, or do you have to go wake them? This was one of the oddest things I found about having a dog who can't hear. She makes herself cozy in the middle of my bed while I'm out running errands.

Do flashes of light, or shadows, frighten your dog? We talked about this in Chapter 6. Lights are translated as loud sounds to your deaf dog.

In older dogs, some of the signs may be different.

Do they seem to be ignoring you? Do they not come when they are called, in particular when they can't see you?

Oscar does this all of the time, but it's because he's stubborn and not deaf. Believe me. I had the vet check.

Are they harder to wake up using noise or calling their name? Do you find you have to nudge them gently?

Do they still meet you at the door when you return home? Or do you have to find them in the house?

Have they become more anxious or more easily startled?

Have they stopped being so frightened of things that once freaked them out? For example, the most terrifying creature of all canine life....the vacuum cleaner?

40% of all dogs are afraid of the vacuum cleaner. Why? Well, let's look at it from their point of view.

When a dog sees something new, he will give it a sniff. This vacuum cleaner breed of dog wants to sniff everything very aggressively. The loud noise and vibration are enough to startle anyone, but you forget about your dog's keen sense of smell. It's in complete overdrive while the vacuum is pulling out old forgotten scents trapped in the fabrics of your carpets. It's no wonder that most see it as a predator.

DEAF DOG

59

A dog that once was able to hear, but is struggling now, may appear distressed when you are not where they can see you. Your dog's ears may move around a lot in an effort to hear something. Distressed behavior could also present as their head flicking from side to side, trotting in circles, and being stuck to you like glue to ensure you are still there.

One of the best ways to test this at home is to ring a bell or jingle your car keys near your dog when it is asleep. If your dog doesn't react to it, you may have a dog who can not hear.

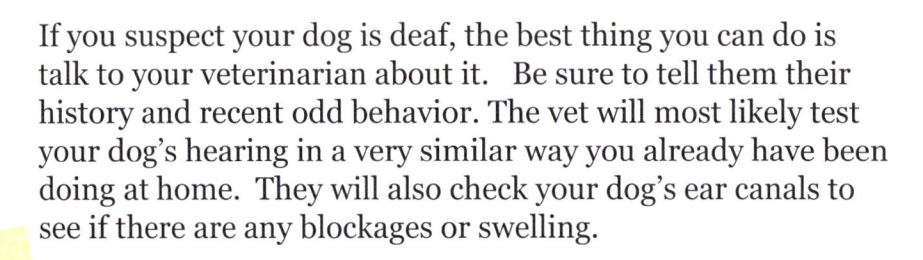

If you suspect your dog is deaf, the best thing you can do is talk to your veterinarian about it. Be sure to tell them their history and recent odd behavior. The vet will most likely test your dog's hearing in a very similar way you already have been doing at home. They will also check your dog's ear canals to see if there are any blockages or swelling.

Some vets also can administer a test called the Brainstem Auditory Evoked Response Test (BAER). This will measure your dog's brain activity in response to various sounds. It is usually a costly test, and not many vets have access to the equipment.

Our vet stood behind our dog and snapped his fingers near her head. When she didn't respond, he asked us to bring her back so he could try a dog whistle. A few days later, he tried that. She didn't act like she could hear it at all, but every other dog in their office went crazy!

DEAF DOG

How can I treat deafness in an older dog?
Remember the old saying, "You can't teach an old dog new tricks?" Well, I'm going to enlighten you. It is NOT true. Yes, you can teach them new tricks! And believe it or not, they will pick up using American Sign Language just like a puppy would.

Remember to sign as you speak to them. They should pick it up rather quickly and begin to adjust to their new method of communication.

Of course, every dog is different, and every situation is different. A dog can also suffer from dementia, problems with their sight, etc.

Always consult a veterinarian with any concerns with your pet.

River Roo discovered this frog on the window one evening. I simply pointed at it and signed, "frog."

Now, I can point to the window and ask her if she sees a frog there. She will run over and check before returning her observations to me.

Deaf dogs will notice things before dogs who can hear. Without the aid of hearing, they depend more on their other senses.

DEAF DOG

Chapter 9: The Science behind the why?

Why are so many deaf dogs white?
Simply put, it's because of a gene they carry. It will affect both their hearing and their fur color.

Now, as my son say, I will "Mom-xplain."

Dogs that carry a gene known as "piebald" are often unable to hear. Piebaldism results from the absence of melanocytes, which are the cells that create the pigment melanin.

Hang on, "melanin?"

You've probably heard of this in High School Health and Biology because humans have it, too. Melanin is a natural skin pigment. Our hair, skin, and eye color depends on the type and amount of melanin we have. Special skin cells called melanocytes make melanin.

Everyone has the same number of melanocytes, but some people produce more melanin than others.

Same with dogs. It's what drives their fur to be a particular color.

Congenital Deafness or deaf from birth
It is estimated that 5-10% of dogs in the United States cannot hear in either one or both ears.

Hereditary Deafness
Cochleosaccular: most common cause of deafness and is associated with coat color patterns. It is usually seen in dogs with the piebald color genes or merle color genes. It can cause deafness in either one or both ears and is seen more in association with blue eyes and a white coat.

This type of deafness can be first seen between 1 to 3 weeks of age.

Neuroepithelial.: not associated with coat patterns. It usually impacts both ears and is typically seen around the same age

There other causes of hearing loss, too.

62   DEAF DOG

The ability to hear is made possible by a particular layer of cells inside the inner ear. This layer of cells, and the cells that determine a dog's hair color, come from the same stem cell source. Dogs that lack this stem cell won't make this layer of hearing cells and will likely be white in coloration. Often, blue eyes will also result.

Little is known about the prevalence of deafness in dogs carrying the pigment merle gene. Studies show that they test between 0.9-2.7% being deaf.

According to ongoing studies, Dalmatians are reported as the most affected by congenital deafness, with reports as high as 34% Unilaterally (deaf in both) ears.

Get that? 34%!

Think back to that old Disney movie, 101 Dalmations. According to this number, 34 of those puppies should have been over in a corner signing to each other.

Dogs of any breed can be deaf from various causes, both hereditary and acquired.

Some breeds seem to have more of an occurrence of congenital deafness.

See pages 64 for a full list.

Some breeds affected by congentional deafness

- 34 % Dalmation
- 21 % Bull Terrier
- 12 % English Sitter
- 15 % Australian Cattle Dog
- 7 %   Cocker Spaniel

Always consult your vet if you suspect ANY strange or unusual behavior from your pet.

True Story.
I realized I hadn't had to fuss at him for two complete days. I took him to the vet and discovered he had an ear infection.

Something is wrong! Oscar has been such a good boy!

DEAF DOG

Dog Breeds with Reported Congenital Deafness

Akita	Cocker Spaniel	Newfoundland Landseer
Alapaha Blue Blood Bulldog / Otto Bulldog	Collie	Norwegian Duckerhound
	Coton de Tulear	Nova Scotia Duck Tolling Retriever
American Bulldog	Dalmatian	Old English Sheepdog
American-Canadian Shepherd	Dappled Dachshund	Papilon
	Doberman Pinscher	Pekingese
American Eskimo	Dogo Argentino	Perro de carca Leones
American Hairless Terrier	English Bulldog	Pit Bull Terrier
Anatolian Shepherd	English Cocker Spaniel	Pointer / English Pointer
Australian Cattle Dog	English Setter	Presa Canario
Australian Kelpie	Foxhound	Puli
Australian Shepherd	Fox Terrier	Rhodesian Ridgeback
Australian Stumpy-tail Cattle Dog	French Bulldog	Rat Terrier
	German Shepherd	Rottweiler
Beagle	German Shorthaired Pointer	Sainte Brrnacrd
Belgian Sheepdog / Groenendael	Goldendoodle	Saluki
	Great Dane	Samoyed
Belgian Tervuren	Great Pyrene	Schauzer
Bichon Frise	Greater Swiss Mountain Dog	Scttish Terrier
Border Collie	Greyhound	Sealhamd Terrier
Borzoi	Havanese	Shetland Sheepdog
Boston Terrier	Ibizan Hound	Shih Tza
Boxer	Icelandic Sheepdog	Shropshire Terrier
Brittany Spaniel	Italian Greyhound	Siverian Husky
Bulldog	Jack / Parson Russell Terrier	Soft Coated Wheaten Terrier
Bullmastiff	Japanese Chin	Springer Spaniel
Bull Terrier	Kangal Shepherd Dog	Susses Spaniel
Carann Dog	Keeshond	Tibetan Spaniel
Cardian Welsh Corgi	Kuvasz	Tibetan Terrier
Catahoula Leopard Dog	Labrador Retriever	Toy Fox Terrier
Catalan Shepherd	Lhasa Apso	Toy Poodle
Cavalier King Charles Spaniel Chihuahua	Lowchen	Walker American Foxhound
	Maltese	West Highland White Terrier
Chinese Crested	Manchester Terrier	Whippet
Chow Chow	Miniature Pinscher Mongrel	Yorkshire Terrier

Dogs of any breed can have congenital deafness, from various causes, both hereditary and acquired.

Breeds with white pigmentation are most often affected.

Chapter 10

Signing with one hand
"Mom-xplained"

A friend of mine asked me, "How can you use sign language without the use of both hands? I mean, if I'm walking my dog on a leash, I'm holding the leash in one hand, and I'll be unable to sign."

It's a valid question that I felt not only needed to be answered but explained.

People who use American Sign Language don't always have both hands-free while talking about something. When that happens, they use their dominant hand when signing. (Well, honestly. It's alright to use either hand.)

For example:

To the right, you will see me signing one of River's favorite things, bacon.

Yes, that's two hands, but what if I'm cooking with one?

Now, look here.

This sign is also the word "bacon."

I just used one hand and got the same meaning across.

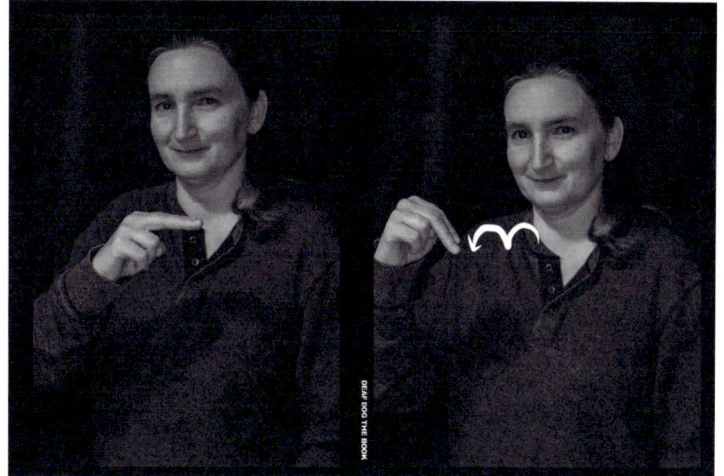

DEAF DOG   65

It's very simple. All words, well most words, are easily recognizable when you just sign half of them. For the purposes that we're using ASL for, it will be just fine.

Here is another example.

I'm making the sign for "bone" or "bones."

I'm signing "bone" again, but with one hand.

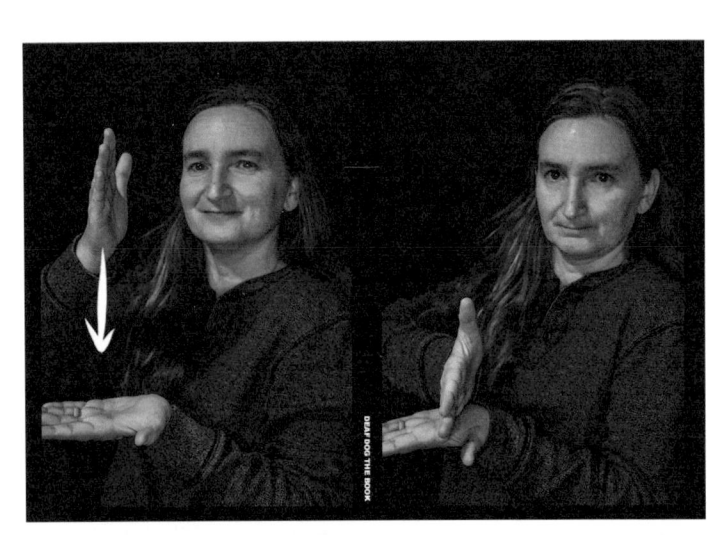

Another example.

One you're more likely to use. Here you can see me signing, "Stop."

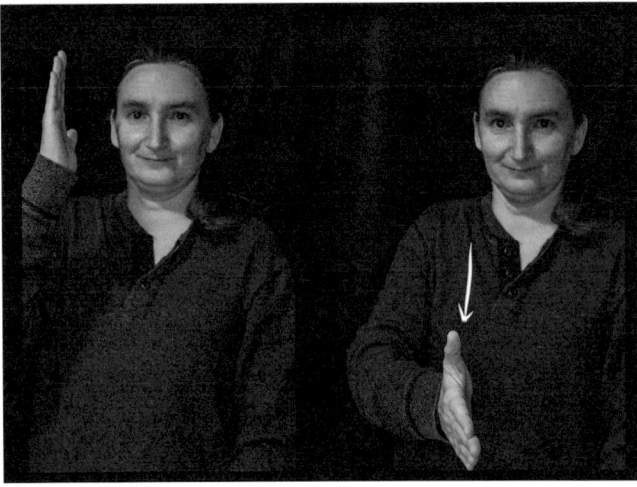

And here it is again. "Stop" with one hand.

Like many owners of deaf dogs, we use a vibrating collar to call River Roo back. But, let's imagine that moment when she doesn't come back when she's called. You walk around the yard, search everywhere, but still, you don't see her or hear her bark.

Notice what I typed there? HEAR her bark.

The idea of someone falling into a hole and shouting for help is so strong that we would naturally assume that's what would happen in this case.

I call the dog.

"Woof! I'm here."

As an owner of a deaf dog, you have to adjust your thinking. She's not going to call out for help. She doesn't think that way. She's never heard anyone shout, speak, whisper, or make a sound. The idea that she would bark because she's being called is not a natural response for her.

River Roo and I climbed into our empty swimming pool to make our point. (Okay, she may have fallen in and I may have almost never got out because I'm shorter than a coffee-table gremlin.)

Jesus, send a ladder!

#Imayhavehadtocallforhelp #whodoyoucall #shortproblems #deafdogthebook #deafdogowner #whataday #MomLife #atleastitwas #empty #drypool #RiverRoo #deafdog #moibaby #allsmiles #shortMomma #wemadeitout #safeaboveground #betterideas #AmericanSignLanguage #newwordswerelearned #short #tallwall #ladder #polevault #alienabduction #howarewegettingout #isthehusbandworkinglate #bettercallaneighbor #Friday #deafdogsrock

DEAF DOG

I'm having trouble keeping my dog's attention. She won't look at me, and so she is not seeing me sign to her. How can I make her look at me long enough to sign something to her?

Believe me. I feel your pain. My deaf dog will often be so distracted because she's playing or on such high alert that she doesn't care what I have to say to her. And if she's not looking at me, why even bother signing? Thankfully, this situation is easier than you think. Get yourself two of your dog's favorite treats and hold them while you sign. Trust me. That will get everyone in your pack's attention!

ATTENTION ALL DOGS

Getting a good scratchy is something that is grossly overlooked in today's society. It costs nothing and benefits both you and your dog owner in many ways.

DON'T YOU LOVE TO SEE THEM HAPPY? IF ONLY THEY HAD A TAIL TO WAG!

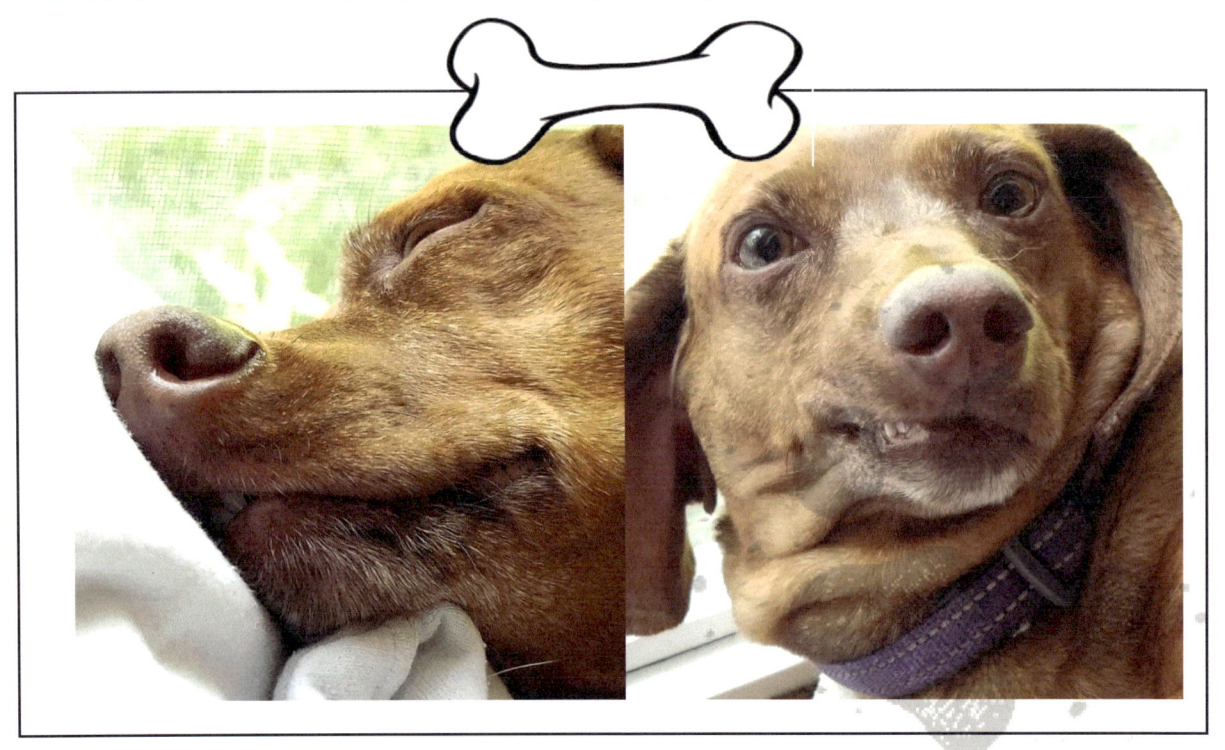

DEAF DOG

Chapter 11: Let's talk about Shedding

Most dogs who are deaf will have a white coat of fur. You will be able to see their hair quickly. Not only the hair on your dog but the hair that falls off. It gets on everything. Seriously. Every corner of your home, your backseat, your lovely black dress. It's like living in a snowglobe.

When we first adopted River, her fur would fog around her whenever she just walked by us. It turns out that she had a vitamin deficiency from being fed some cheap dog food. As soon as she got some good grub, she did a bit better.

Our veterinarian also had us give her fish oil daily for a while. We just put a squirt of it on her food before we gave it to her. It helped a little.

When she began to get more comfortable with us, and her anxiety reduced. So did her shedding.

She started getting bathed regularly at our groomers. I mentioned the excess shedding, and they used a special shampoo on River. That helped a lot, too.

> "Mom. I thought this was a book about a dog being deaf. Not about a dog being a dog!"
> - Opinionated teenager.

> "Mom. I don't think it's "River" has all this hair. Instead, it should be, "we all" have all of this hair. I think we are probably expelling it as we breathe."
> - Good observation of a teenager.

If only I could think of a good use for all of that dog hair…. hmm. See page 120

DEAF DOG

69

Actual image of my husband blowing River's dog hair out of our car with a leaf blower. Who can relate?

POOF!!

C. Bender

As you can see, it wasn't just one factor that contributed to me signing to River that she was "Mommy's little powdered donut." Not only is she mixed with some breed that has an undercoat, but she also lives in the Southern United States, where the humidity will make you feel like you are baking in your own skin.

Imagine how a dog wearing a fur coat feels in that humidity. Woo. I'd rather not even think about it.

Growing up in the Appalachian Mountains, our grandparents had us actually scratch our dogs before the days of smartphones or computers.

I don't mean an occasional pat or a little scratch as you pass by. No. I'm talking about sitting down in a chair, calling your dog over to yourself, and spending the next twenty or so minutes scratching your dog.

As a parent, I know this is because we were annoying little kids, and they were just looking for something to keep us busy for a few minutes so they could have some peace and quiet. But, as a dog owner, I see where this actually has helped River with her shedding more than anything else has.

No one can tell us when, where, or why this proud, honorable, and very old tradition began. But, not to worry. I have decided to educate you on the proper technique of the "Good ole Fashioned Southern Dawg Scratching."

First things first, find your dog and fix yourself a tall glass of sweet tea. Mountain knowledge is about to be passed down to another generation of dog owners.

Old Fashioned SOUTHERN DAWG SCRATCHING

Step 1: Take your dog outside cause you are about to get a lot of their hair fogging around. You don't want to do this in the house.

Sit on the edge of a chair, placing your varmint directly between your legs.

Crack your knuckles and send your child inside to refill your tea. You're going to need it. (My particular recipe is on page 91.

Step 2: Start at your dog's neck and work your way down her back. Think about how itchy their hair is when it accidentally gets on you! Imagine if it was all over you like it is them!

Massage and scratch behind their ears. Your dog's ears are loaded with nerve endings. Rubbing them will increase her production of endorphins, the feel-good hormone.

The best way to rub her ears is to start nearest to the head and grasp it firmly but gently.

Scratch and massage up and down her back. You should see the hair beginning to bunch up. Just pick it up, and knock it to the ground.

DEAF DOG

Step 3: By now, your other dogs are probably protesting that you are giving one all of the attention. Tell them to wait their turn or draft a nearby child to scratch them.

Want them to do a great job? Tell them you'll pay $5 to whoever gets the larger pile of hair. This was the game of my youth. Who can get the biggest pile of dog hair?

After about five minutes of this, take a break and drink your sweet tea. This is "dog scratching half-time."

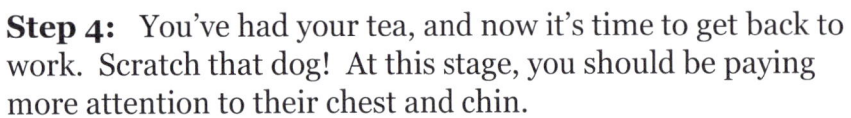

Step 4: You've had your tea, and now it's time to get back to work. Scratch that dog! At this stage, you should be paying more attention to their chest and chin.

This dog is putty in your hands right now. Discuss with them things like squirrels, politics, family drama, or anything that works you up. Take out all of that frustration in that scratching! Our grandparents used this is an anti-depressant!

Step 5: At some point, your dog will roll over and want you to scratch her tummy. Many dogs like to start with this and will roll over anytime you mention, "Scratchy!"

Continue until you have gotten a bunch of hair off of your dog. You'll be amazed at how much a quick 10-minute job will help with shedding.

Be sure to wear clothes you don't mind getting furry. I probably should have started with that. Sorry.

A scratch reflex is often seen when you give your dog a "Good ole Fashioned Southern Dawg Scratching."

For most dogs, this happens when you scratch their stomach, hind leg, or the base of their spine. Not only is it cute, but it also serves a purpose. Those are locations of nerve clusters that protect dogs from ticks, fleas, or other critters that may irritate their skin. These nerves send a message to the hind leg, via the spinal cord, to start kicking to dislodge whatever irritates the skin.

Veterinarians use this reflex to check dogs for nerve or neurological damage. The same way that human doctors test our reflexes by hitting the patellar tendon at our knee.

The dog scratch reflex insightful into your dog's neurological health and is also extremely entertaining to their owner.

You'll see the silliest faces, hear the craziest noises, and laugh more than you ever thought. I would recommend having your camera ready!

Give it a try!

Salty Dog

Look for ways to give your fur baby a 10-15 minute scratch throughout your day. My favorite position is when I'm working on the computer,

C. Bender

DEAF DOG

73

Chapter 12

Things that I never expected

My husband's awesome ideas usually work out for the best. Even though I was apprehensive about it, River makes a beautiful addition to our family.

River and Oscar are inseparable. I think that River may believe she is also a Dachshund. She loves to burrow into her blankets as he does. She will jump into your lap, thinking she's much smaller of a dog than she is.

But, if River has decided she wants to be a Dachshund, we'll accept her and love her just the same.

My husband has learned some sign language. Although, the way he remembers these things are just strange.

One evening, he was cooking some steaks on the grill. Our dogs supervised and drooled as the delicious aroma filled their lungs.

My husband asked me how to sign the word "steak."

After I showed him, he smiled. "Well, that makes sense."

"Does it? Why?"

"That's how you test to make sure steak is done."

Y'all. I had never heard of this mess. I googled it and thanked the good Lord when I saw that it was a thing. Here I was worried that I had married Jeffery Dahmer. Google it if you want to know exactly how it is done, but basically, it looks just like this sign.

74

DEAF DOG

Our deaf dog loves to go camping with us. Because River can't hear when the small children wake up, she sleeps in!

River Roo associates camping with free hot dogs.

She manages to steal them from anyone we're camping with. So, if you see us someday on a campsite, come up and say hi. But, keep two eyes on your hot dogs. If River doesn't grab them, her brother Oscar totally will!

> *"Mom. River is just over there! Sign louder!"*
> *- Brain dead teenager.*

INT. – OUR FAMILY LIVING ROOM – NIGHT

A mom sits in a cozy chair, drinking a hot cup of tea. She's looked forward to this one moment of peace all day. She picks up the remote control and turns on the television.

After she has sat just long enough to get a well-worn butt print on the cushion, her dog OSCAR MAYER looks up at her and whines. TWO MORE DOGS lay on a bean bag, watching television.

                MOM
       (signs) Dang it. I just sat down!

         OSCAR'S PUPPY DOG EYES
    I'm so sorry, Mom. But, I have to pee.

The mom groans and sits down her cup. As she begins to stand up, she looks over to see her husband, DE MAN. He is comfortable in his cozy leather chair. He hasn't noticed what has been going on because he has fallen into a Facebook Rabbit Hole. She sees that he hasn't taken off his shoes and smiles as she sits back down.

                MOM
   (signs) Hey. Tell Dad you need to outside, and he'll give you a piece of delicious steak.

            ALL DOGS
       (flip completely out)

             DE MAN
    What the hell is their problem?

                MOM
   I have no idea! They've been like that all day.

DE MAN stands up and walks with the dogs jumping all over him to open the door.

             DE MAN
   (grumbles) Come on, you guys. I swear. All I have to do is sit down in front of you, and everybody suddenly has to pee.

MOM hides her smile behind her hot cup of tea.

DEAF DOG

DEAF DOG

My favorite teenager signing, "I love you" to me as he goes to class.

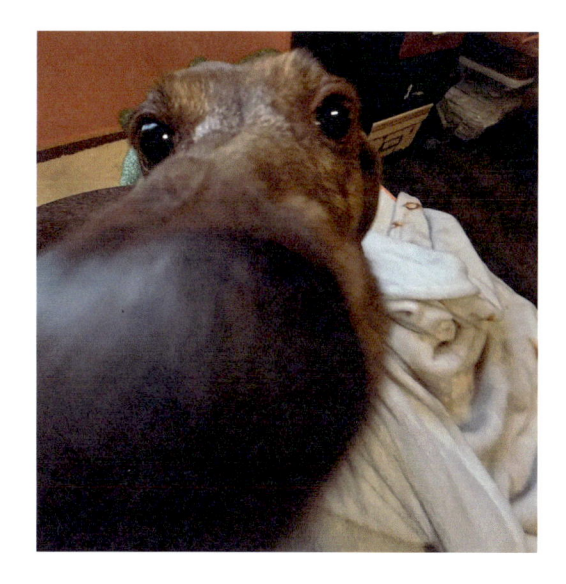

Our "needing an elective" high school teenager has now taken two American Sign Language courses to learn to talk more with his dog. Isn't that crazy?

Isn't that amazing?

River came from the pound to living with someone who loves her enough to learn a complete, new language. Just, so they can teach it to her. That's rather awesome.

Everyone deserves a home like that.

When I first thought of writing this book, my reason was to help a family thinking about adopting a dog, possibly giving a deaf dog a chance. But, now that I've reached the end of this project, I pray that it does more than that. I had no idea how many dogs are euthanized because they are unable to hear. That's it—the only reason.

That's outrageous.

People. Do better.

If this book saves one life, it will be worth more than any amount of time I've put into it. Think about adopting a deaf dog. They will teach you how to hear with your heart.

DEAF DOG

The Alphabet in American Sign Language

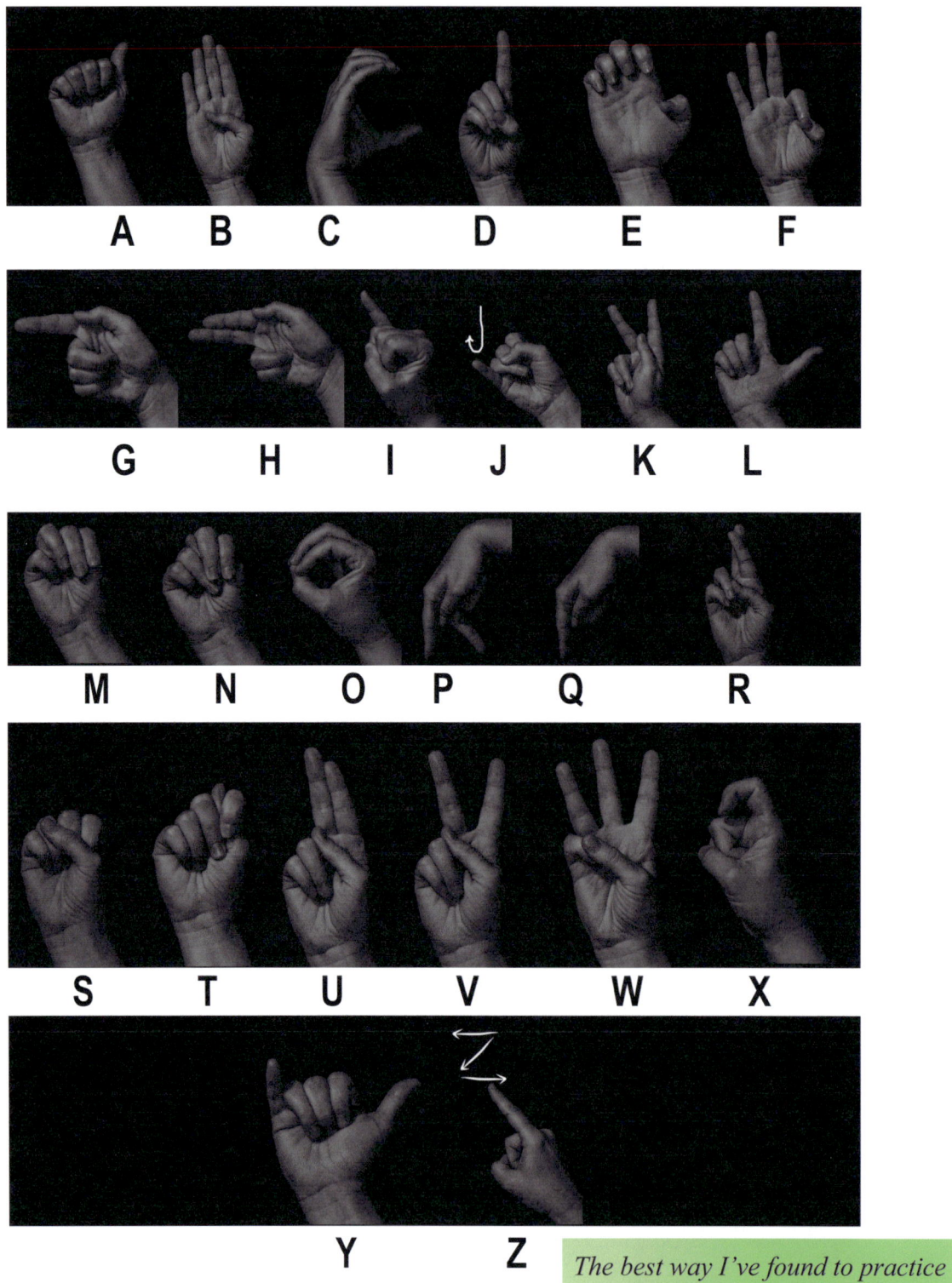

A B C D E F

G H I J K L

M N O P Q R

S T U V W X

Y Z

The best way I've found to practice "finger spelling" is while I drive. Spell the names of the roads, or anything else you can think of!

American Sign Language Dictionary

Angry

Your expression is your tone of voice.

☐ I know this sign
☐ My dog knows this sign

Applause
Wave your hands beside your face. Think, "Jazz Hands!"

You want to get your point across using the least amount of signs. That's true whether you are signing to your dog or a deaf person.

☐ I know this sign
☐ My dog knows this sign

Baby
Cradle your hand in your other one as if you are cradling a baby.
I often tell our deaf dog that she's my baby.

*Examples of what to sign:
My - Baby - You
Mom Baby
Where your baby?*

☐ I know this sign
☐ My dog knows this sign

DEAF DOG 79

American Sign Language Dictionary

Bacon
Think about what bacon looks like when you make this sign.

DOG FAVORITE

☐ I know this sign
☐ My dog knows this sign

Bad
Extend your hand from your face, then flip it over.

Your expression is your tone of voice.

☐ I know this sign
☐ My dog knows this sign

Ball
Make a round shape with your hands.

We also use this for the word "Fetch."

Examples of what to sign:
Play - Ball
Where - Ball
Mom - Ball
(Bring Mom the ball)

☐ I know this sign
☐ My dog knows this sign

American Sign Language Dictionary

Bath
Make fists with your thumbs popped out, and rub your chest as if you are soaping up in the bath.

Don't expect your dog to like this sign. Ours run from it.

Examples of what to sign:
You - Bath
Brother - Bath
Where - Brother - Bath

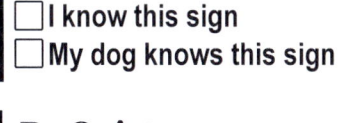

☐ I know this sign
☐ My dog knows this sign

Be Quiet
Use the simple "finger over the lips" that we all learn as children.

Interestingly enough, this was the first sign our deaf dog saw us sign to her. And it was my husband who did it! He didn't realize it was the same sign. As you further your study on ASL, you will realize you actually know more than you think you did.

☐ I know this sign
☐ My dog knows this sign

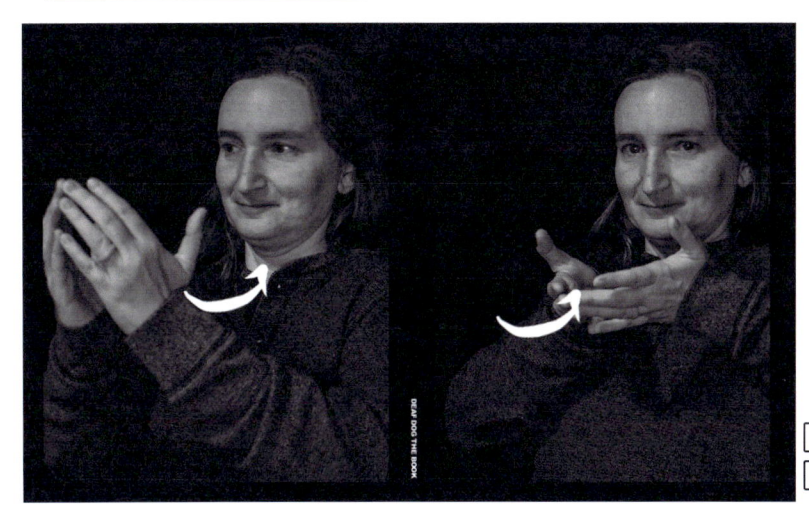

Boat
Cup your hands together and move them closer to your chest as shown. Think of the keel of a boat.

☐ I know this sign
☐ My dog knows this sign

DEAF DOG

American Sign Language Dictionary

Bone
Two fingers, like shown, then curl them.

Examples of what to sign:
(Name) - Want - Bone
Where - Bone
(Name) - Bone

DOG FAVORITE

☐ I know this sign
☐ My dog knows this sign

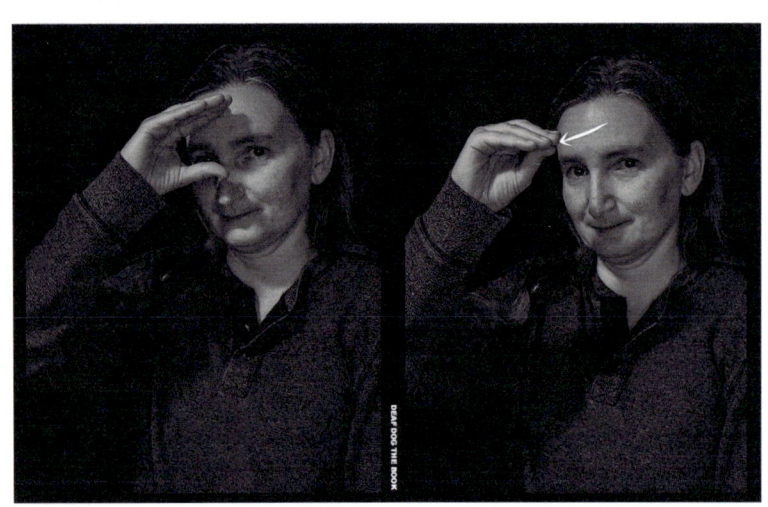

Boy
Think of a cap or a hat like baseball players wear. That's an easy way to remember this sign.

☐ I know this sign
☐ My dog knows this sign

Brother
First sign, "Boy," then add the last step.

☐ I know this sign
☐ My dog knows this sign

82 DEAF DOG

American Sign Language Dictionary

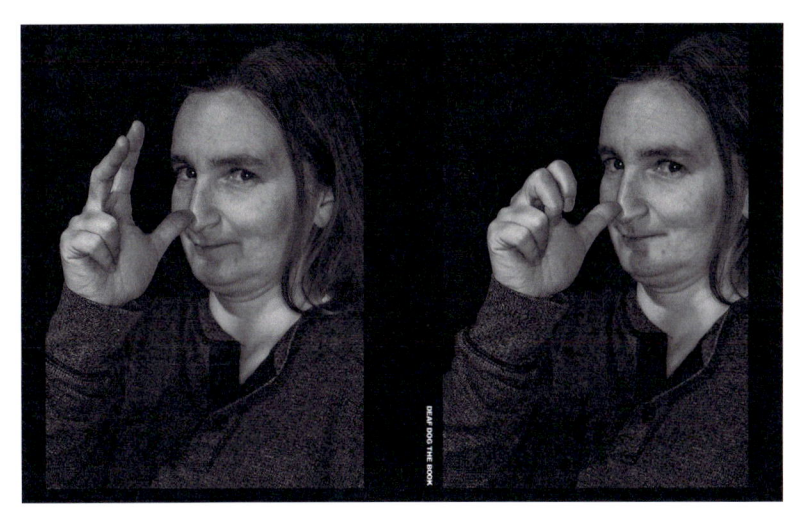

Bug, Tick, Flea
This sign always reminds me of the antenna bugs have. That's an excellent way to remember it.

Camp, Camping
Extend your index fingers and pinkies to make what looks like tent poles.

Examples of what to sign:
(Name) - Like - Camp
Go - Camping
Go - Camper

DOG FAVORITE

☐ I know this sign
☐ My dog knows this sign

Careful, Be Careful
Make a "k" with both of your hands. Stack them and then move this back and forth.

Remember, to sign this one-handed, use your dominant hand.

Your expression is your tone of voice.

☐ I know this sign
☐ My dog knows this sign

DEAF DOG 83

American Sign Language Dictionary

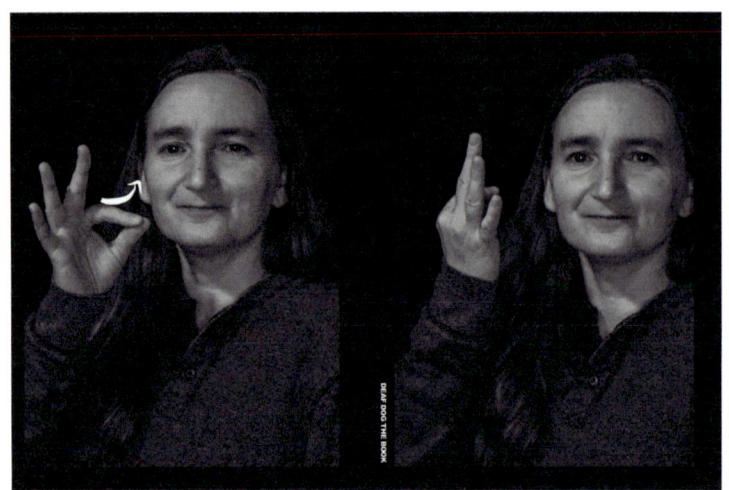

Cat
This sign makes me think of the whiskers of a cat.

Did you know that the older a cat (or dog) gets, the longer its whiskers grow?

☐ I know this sign
☐ My dog knows this sign

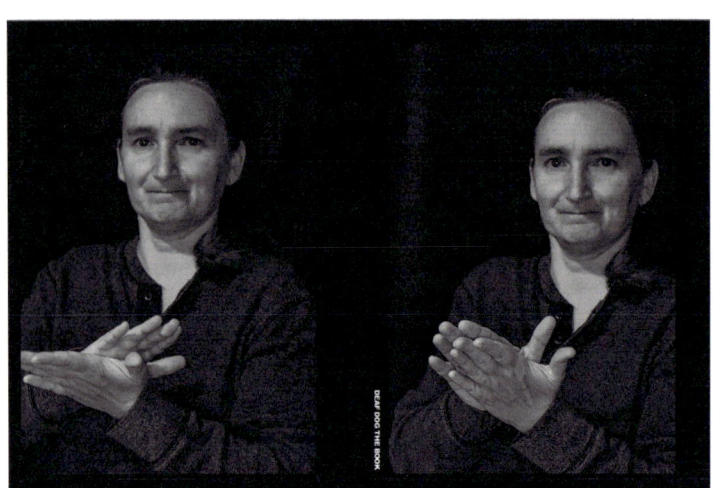

Cheese
See this sign? It looks like I'm cutting the cheese.

"Cutting the cheese." Ha!

☐ I know this sign
☐ My dog knows this sign

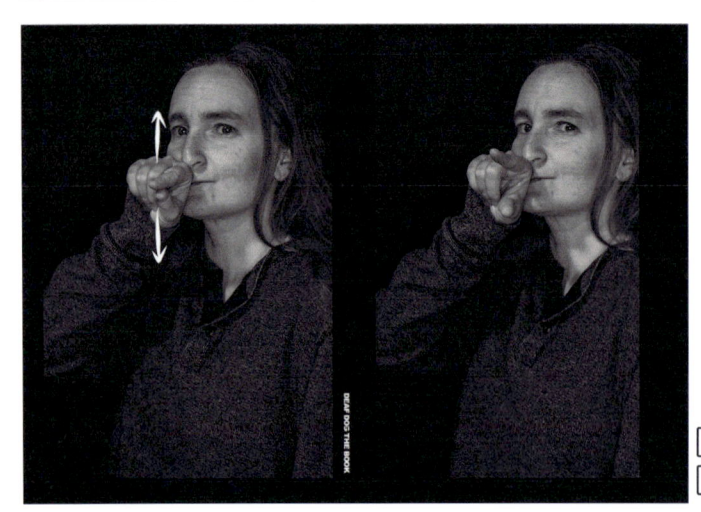

Chicken
It's a beak!
Like a chicken has!

Examples of what to sign:
Where - Chicken
Like - Chicken
Hungry - Chicken

☐ I know this sign
☐ My dog knows this sign

American Sign Language Dictionary

Clean
This is similar to the sign for cheese. But, your top hand doesn't change direction as it does for the other sign. Just keep it straight here and move it across your other palm.

☐ I know this sign
☐ My dog knows this sign

Cold
Hold your fists close to your body and move them as if you are shivering.

Your expression is your tone of voice.

☐ I know this sign
☐ My dog knows this sign

Collar
I sign this to our deaf dog when I want her to come to me to put her on her electric collar.

*Examples of what to sign:
Come home - Collar
Where is - Your - Collar?
Bath - Collar*

☐ I know this sign
☐ My dog knows this sign

DEAF DOG

American Sign Language Dictionary

Cookie
Twist your top hand around as if you are turning a cookie.

☐ I know this sign
☐ My dog knows this sign

Crazy
How about that? You already knew a sign and didn't even realize it.

Your expression is your tone of voice.

☐ I know this sign
☐ My dog knows this sign

Cute
Two fingers on your chin, and then move them down.

Examples of what to sign:
Cute - Girl / Boy
Cute - Dog
Pretty - Cute - Favorite - Dog

☐ I know this sign
☐ My dog knows this sign

DEAF DOG

American Sign Language Dictionary

Dad, Father, Papa
All five fingers extended as you put your thumb to your head.

Examples of what to sign:
Play - Dad
Where - Dad
Dad - Work / Home

☐ I know this sign
☐ My dog knows this sign

Dance
We are always minutes from starting a dance party in our house.

☐ I know this sign
☐ My dog knows this sign

Dead
You would be surprised how often I have to sign this.
"River, don't bring that squirrel in here. It's dead!"

☐ I know this sign
☐ My dog knows this sign

DEAF DOG 87

American Sign Language Dictionary

Dirty
Wiggle your fingers under your chin.

Your expression is your tone of voice.

☐ I know this sign
☐ My dog knows this sign

Dog
The word in ASL is a little different than this, but someone who is deaf will recognize this as "dog," too.

☐ I know this sign
☐ My dog knows this sign

Doll
Move your index finger down the bridge of your nose.

☐ I know this sign
☐ My dog knows this sign

American Sign Language Dictionary

Donut
Crossed fingers, then make a half circle with them. As if you are outlining a donut.

☐ I know this sign
☐ My dog knows this sign

Drive, Car, Ride
Move your hands back and forth as if you are steering the car.

Examples of what to sign:
Go - Ride?
Go - Car
Ready - Ride - Camp

DOG FAVORITE

☐ I know this sign
☐ My dog knows this sign

Drums
Just imagine you are a drummer on that snare drum. Rat-at-tat-tat.

☐ I know this sign
☐ My dog knows this sign

American Sign Language Dictionary

Eat, Food
Gotta eat, right?

This is a very simple sign that you probably already know.

DOG FAVORITE

☐ I know this sign
☐ My dog knows this sign

Egg
Two fingers, tapped together as if you are breaking an egg. Then, move them to point.

Our dogs love to eat scrambled eggs, and it's good for their coat.

☐ I know this sign
☐ My dog knows this sign

Favorite
Touch your middle finger to your chin.

Your expression is your tone of voice.

☐ I know this sign
☐ My dog knows this sign

90 DEAF DOG

American Sign Language Dictionary

Finished
Make the sign for "F" and then twist it out.

☐ I know this sign
☐ My dog knows this sign

Frog
Place your fist under your chin and then extend a finger, just like a frog does his chin.

☐ I know this sign
☐ My dog knows this sign

"Mom-Mom's" Southern Sweet Iced Tea Recipe

1-gallon water (or 16 cups)
3 black tea bags, some people use more
1 cup of sugar, some people use more or less

Put water in a pot on the stove with the teabags floating around. Turn heat to medium. Before the water comes to a boil, the water will begin to look brown. When it's dark, but not too dark that you can't see through it, it's done.
Turn off heat and allow to cool a bit. Pour into a gallon container and mix sugar while it is still warm. Refrigerate. Serve cold with more than six cubes of ice.

American Sign Language Dictionary

Get out of here!
Believe it or not, I use this sign more with my son's friends than I do with my dogs.

☐ I know this sign
☐ My dog knows this sign

Girl
Move your thumb along your chin. Think about a bonnet that little girls used to wear years ago. That will help you remember this sign.

☐ I know this sign
☐ My dog knows this sign

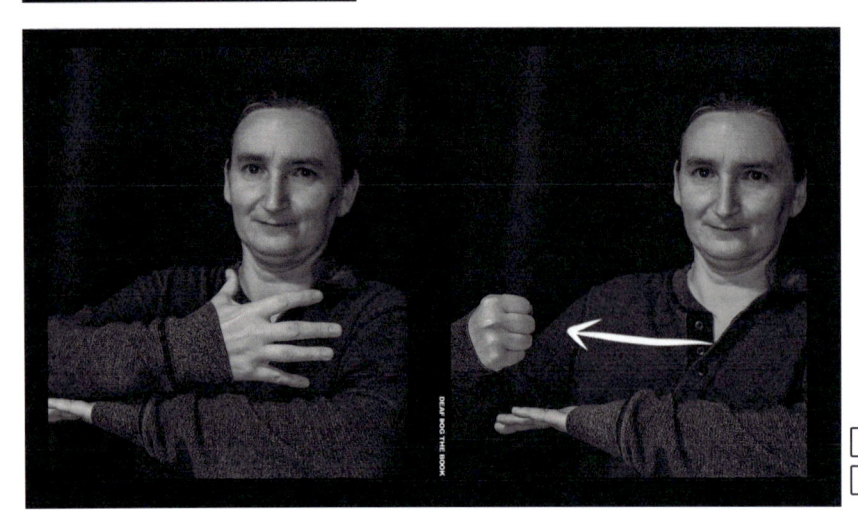

Gone
I usually use this more for food than the sign, "finished." I don't think Oscar ever finishes eating. He just keeps going, going, going, going, going

☐ I know this sign
☐ My dog knows this sign

92   DEAF DOG

American Sign Language Dictionary

Good
Move the palm of your hand outwards.

☐ I know this sign
☐ My dog knows this sign

Hello

Your expression is your tone of voice.

☐ I know this sign
☐ My dog knows this sign

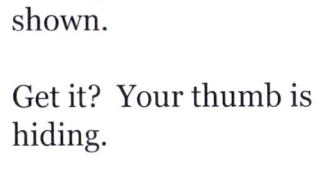

Hide
Move your thumb under your palm as shown.

Get it? Your thumb is hiding.

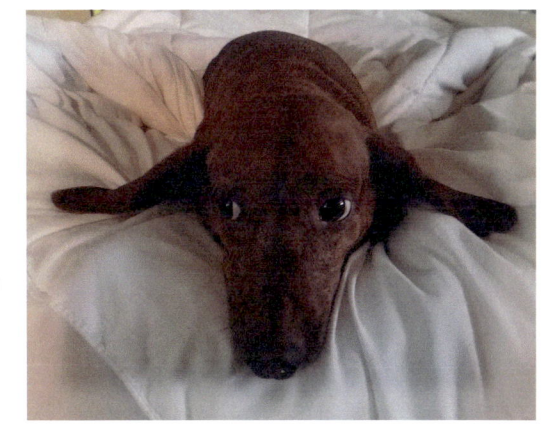

☐ I know this sign
☐ My dog knows this sign

DEAF DOG 93

American Sign Language Dictionary

Home
Tap your cheek with your fingertips.

> *Examples of what to sign:*
> *Go - Home*
> *Home*
> *Go (Car) Home?*

☐ I know this sign
☐ My dog knows this sign

Horse
Think of a horse's ear standing up there.

☐ I know this sign
☐ My dog knows this sign

Hot
Twist your hand from under your chin.

> *Examples of what to sign:*
> *Wait - Food - Hot*
> *Outside - Hot*
> *Food - Hot*
> *Careful - Hot*

☐ I know this sign
☐ My dog knows this sign

American Sign Language Dictionary

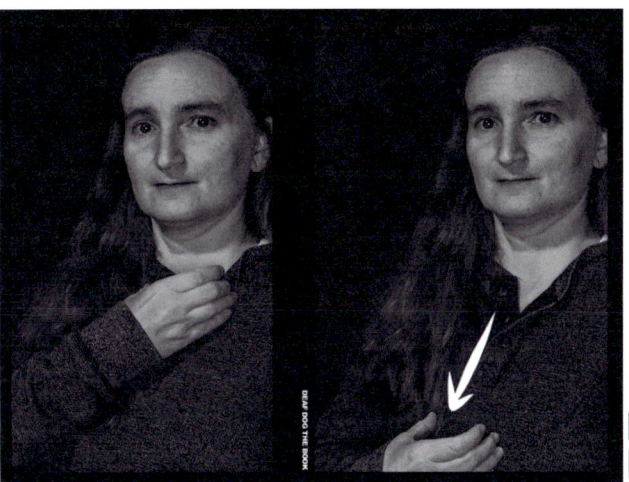

Hungry
Follow your chest down while holding your hand in a "U" shape.

☐ I know this sign
☐ My dog knows this sign

Hunt
Fingers as guns, this is the sign we use when our deaf dog is on high alert for squirrels in our yard.

Your expression is your tone of voice.

☐ I know this sign
☐ My dog knows this sign

Kiss
Just point to your lips.

☐ I know this sign
☐ My dog knows this sign

DEAF DOG

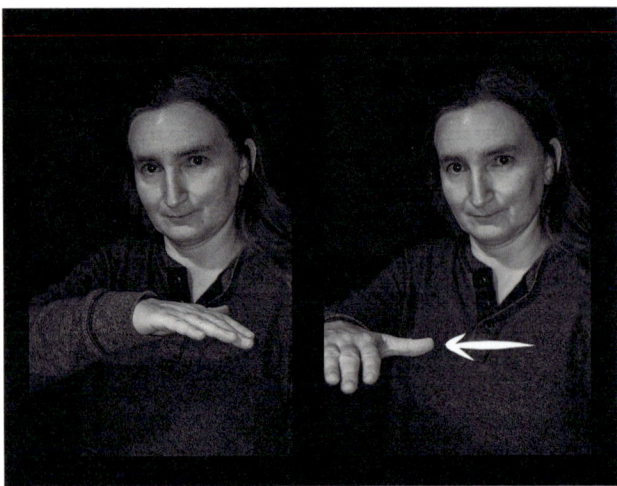

American Sign Language Dictionary

Lie Down
Move your hand smoothly across.

☐ I know this sign
☐ My dog knows this sign

Like
Your thumb and middle finger should touch, and then pull your entire hand back from your chest.

☐ I know this sign
☐ My dog knows this sign

Lizard
This is the sign I use for our bearded dragon.

Examples of what to sign:
See - Lizard?
Lizard - there.
Lizard - not - food.

☐ I know this sign
☐ My dog knows this sign

American Sign Language Dictionary

Long
Move your finger down your arm.

Examples of what to sign:
Not - Time - Long
Tail - Long
Where Doll Tail Long

☐ I know this sign
☐ My dog knows this sign

Love
I hope you use this sign a lot.

Your expression is your tone of voice.

☐ I know this sign
☐ My dog knows this sign

One Minute, Wait

Examples of what to sign:
One Minute - Food - Hot
One Minute
Stop - One Minute

☐ I know this sign
☐ My dog knows this sign

DEAF DOG

American Sign Language Dictionary

Miss
Touch your index finger to your chin.

> *Examples of what to sign:*
> *Mom - Miss - You*
> *I - know - You - Missed - Me*
> *Bye - Miss - You*

☐ I know this sign
☐ My dog knows this sign

Mom
Open your hand with your thumb touching your chin.

"Mom-Mom." Yep. That's me.

☐ I know this sign
☐ My dog knows this sign

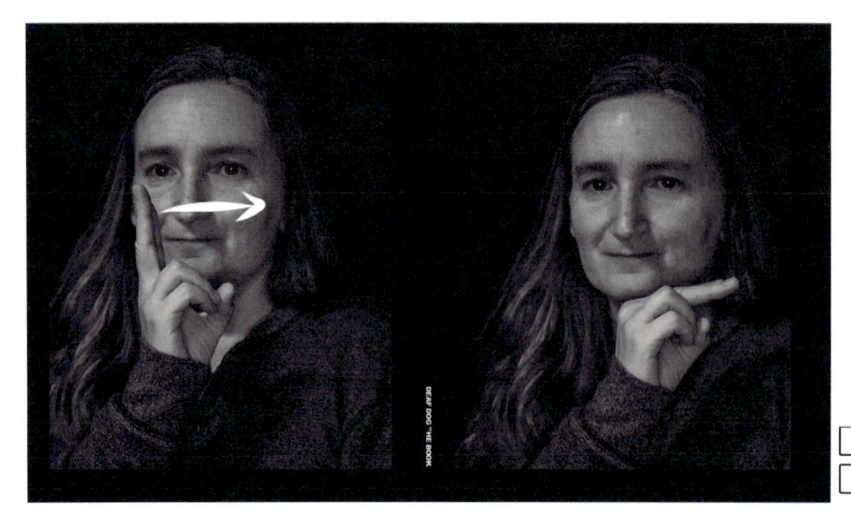

Mouse
There is always a good story to go along with why we have to sign this. Let's just say, "Mom is never this calm when signing this."

☐ I know this sign
☐ My dog knows this sign

DEAF DOG

American Sign Language Dictionary

Movie
I use this when I ask our deaf dog if she would like to watch a movie or when I'm recording a video of her on my phone.

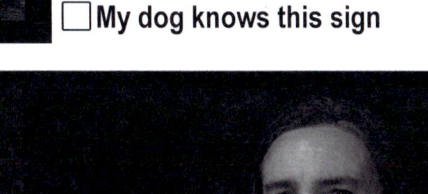

☐ I know this sign
☐ My dog knows this sign

Music, Sing, Song
Think of this as a conductor leading his orchestra.
Move your top hand back and forth.

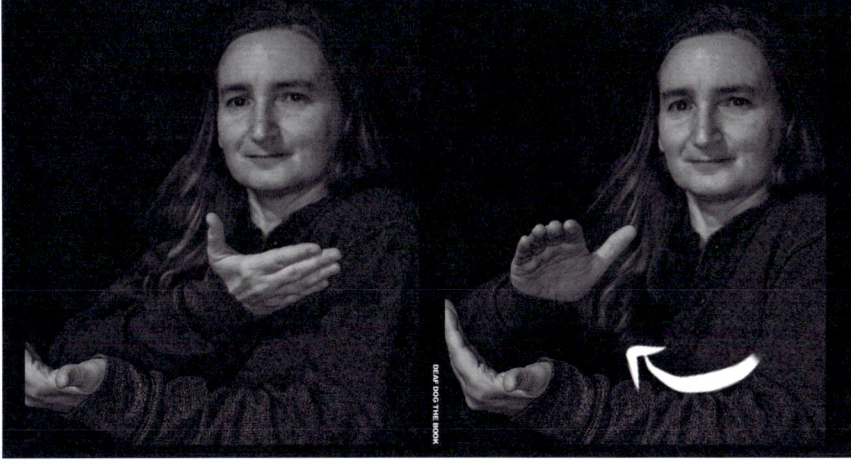

☐ I know this sign
☐ My dog knows this sign

Name
Tap your two fingers on both hands together.

☐ I know this sign
☐ My dog knows this sign

DEAF DOG 99

American Sign Language Dictionary

No
Using your first two fingers, bring them together to your thumb.
I may frame this and put it in my son's bedroom.

Your expression is your tone of voice.

☐ I know this sign
☐ My dog knows this sign

Not
Remember the "no" and "not" story with James in the store with our deaf dog on the loose?

☐ I know this sign
☐ My dog knows this sign

Oatmeal
Imagine scooping up a handful of oatmeal to help you remember this. But, don't be a heathen and use a spoon!

DOG FAVORITE

☐ I know this sign
☐ My dog knows this sign

American Sign Language Dictionary

Picture
Put your hand in a "C" shape and lay it against your face. Then move it to your hand.

☐ I know this sign
☐ My dog knows this sign

Play
Using the "P" in ASL, put your hands beside your face.

DOG FAVORITE

☐ I know this sign
☐ My dog knows this sign

Please
Place your palm on your chest and move it in a circular motion.

What can I say? We're Southern and use manners even with our dog.

☐ I know this sign
☐ My dog knows this sign

DEAF DOG 101

American Sign Language Dictionary

Police
Think of the badge that a police officer wears to help you remember this sign.

☐ I know this sign
☐ My dog knows this sign

Potty, Go Outside
Using the "T" in ASL, raise your hand next to your face.

This is actually the ASL sign for "toilet," but "potty" looks nicer. - Southern Mom.

☐ I know this sign
☐ My dog knows this sign

Powdered
Hold your hand in the C shape and pretend you a shaking a large can.

Our deaf dog sheds more than a powdered donut riding in a convertible.

☐ I know this sign
☐ My dog knows this sign

American Sign Language Dictionary

Pretty, Handsome
Move your hand in a circular motion around your face.

This was the first sign that my grandfather taught me.

☐ I know this sign
☐ My dog knows this sign

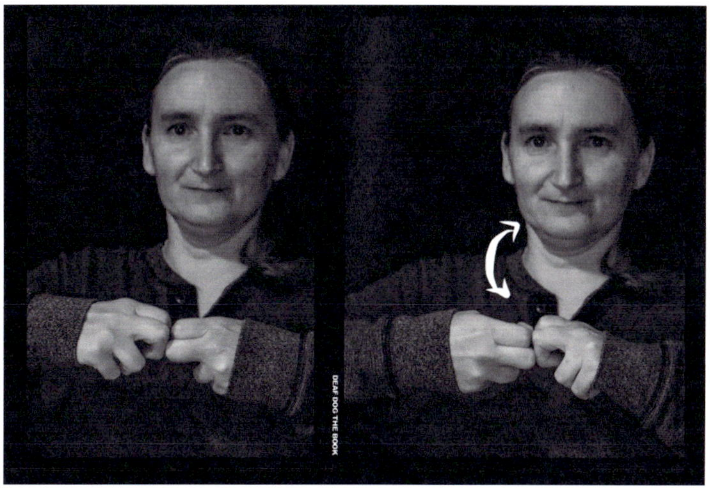

Problem
I use this a lot to ask, "What's your problem?" when they are barking their heads off.

Your expression is your tone of voice.

☐ I know this sign
☐ My dog knows this sign

Rain
Or "banging on the piano." It works for either one. Move your extended fingers up and down quickly.

☐ I know this sign
☐ My dog knows this sign

DEAF DOG

American Sign Language Dictionary

Sausage
Imagine how sausage looks to help you remember this one.

DOG FAVORITE

☐ I know this sign
☐ My dog knows this sign

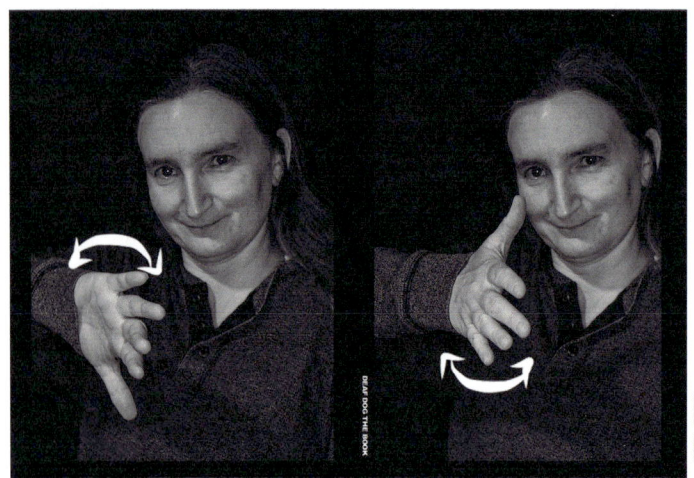

Shake
Twist your palm around quickly.

☐ I know this sign
☐ My dog knows this sign

Sick
Touch your thumb and middle finger together, and tap them on your forehead.

Your expression is your tone of voice.

☐ I know this sign
☐ My dog knows this sign

104 DEAF DOG

American Sign Language Dictionary

Sister
Make the sign for "girl" and then add the extra bit.

☐ I know this sign
☐ My dog knows this sign

Sit
This should be one of the first signs you teach your dog.

☐ I know this sign
☐ My dog knows this sign

Sleep, Bed
Rather easy to remember, you think?

☐ I know this sign
☐ My dog knows this sign

American Sign Language Dictionary

Smile
Using your index fingers, move them up as if you are painting a smile on your face.

☐ I know this sign
☐ My dog knows this sign

Snake
The few times I've ever had to use this, I did not have this expression on my face. Not at all.

☐ I know this sign
☐ My dog knows this sign

Sorry
Spin your fist in a circle on your chest.
I always have to sign this after I've seen a snake. But, somethings just make me forget my good, Christian upbringing.

☐ I know this sign
☐ My dog knows this sign

American Sign Language Dictionary

Squirrel
Imagine your fingers are the teeth of a squirrel eating a nut. Move them up and down.

DOG FAVORITE

☐ I know this sign
☐ My dog knows this sign

Stay
This should be one of the first signs that you teach your dog.

Your expression is your tone of voice.

☐ I know this sign
☐ My dog knows this sign

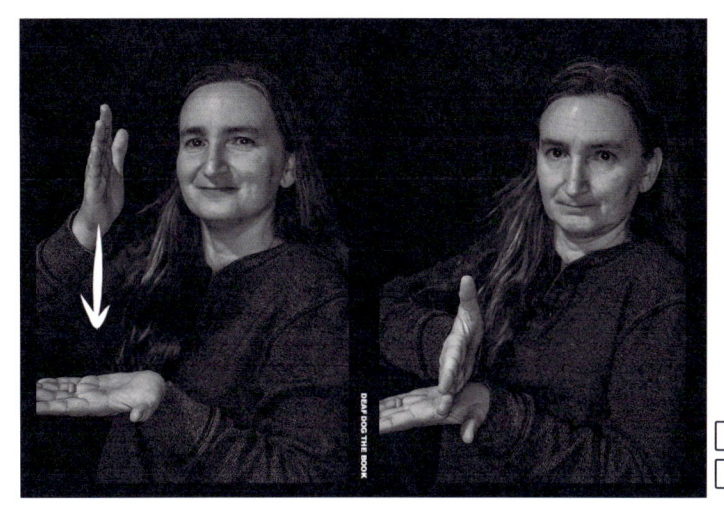

Stop
You can also do this sign, and all of the rest of them, using only your dominant hand.

☐ I know this sign
☐ My dog knows this sign

DEAF DOG

American Sign Language Dictionary

Store
I have seen this where you do as pictured. And another version where you open and close your hands.

☐ I know this sign
☐ My dog knows this sign

Swim, Pool
Always supervise your pet when they are around water.

☐ I know this sign
☐ My dog knows this sign

Taco
Place your hand inside of your other one that is curved.

☐ I know this sign
☐ My dog knows this sign

DEAF DOG

American Sign Language Dictionary

Thirsty
Think about that little tickle you get in your throat that reminds you that you are thirsty. That's an easy way to remember this sign.

Your expression is your tone of voice.

☐ I know this sign
☐ My dog knows this sign

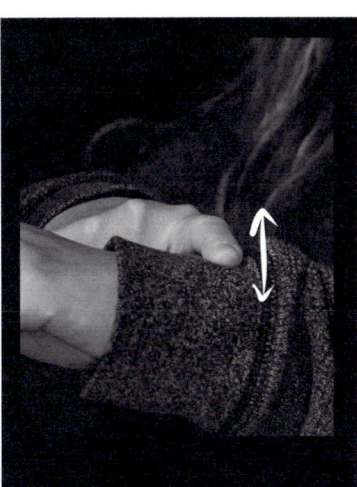

Time
Tap your index finger on your wrist as if you were wearing a wristwatch.

☐ I know this sign
☐ My dog knows this sign

Tired
Holding up your thumbs, turn them down to show that you are tired.

☐ I know this sign
☐ My dog knows this sign

DEAF DOG

American Sign Language Dictionary

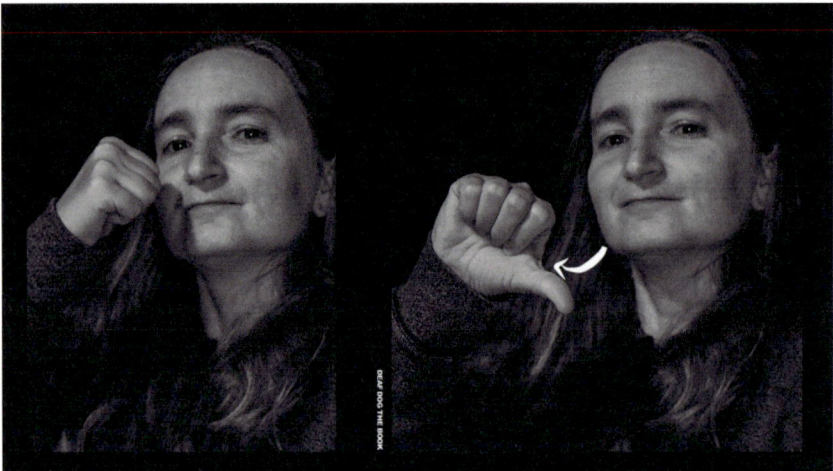

Tomorrow
Place your thumb on your cheek, then twist it down.

☐ I know this sign
☐ My dog knows this sign

Treat
Moving your hands, to and fro', makes your dog long for a treat, and then some mo'.

DOG FAVORITE

☐ I know this sign
☐ My dog knows this sign

Tree
I move my fingers to show the leaves blowing in the wind. It isn't necessary.

☐ I know this sign
☐ My dog knows this sign

American Sign Language Dictionary

Rooster
Remember what a rooster looks like to help you remember this sign.

☐ I know this sign
☐ My dog knows this sign

Vet, Doctor
This is a complex, looking sign. But, do not worry. Just point to your shoulder and make the sign of the cross.
This sign means "Doctor" in ASL, but can be used just fine for our purposes.

☐ I know this sign
☐ My dog knows this sign

Werewolf
Make this motion slowly while using a growling face. I tell my dogs if they eat too many treats, it will turn them into werewolves.

☐ I know this sign
☐ My dog knows this sign

DEAF DOG

American Sign Language Dictionary

Wash
Imagine yourself rubbing soap on yourself to remember this sign.

☐ I know this sign
☐ My dog knows this sign

Water
Tap three fingers to your chin.

☐ I know this sign
☐ My dog knows this sign

> *Oh, and James.*
>
> *In regards that example I talked about where I sign to the dogs to trick you into letting them outside.....*
> *I was just teasing. But, I knew if you asked me about it, it would mean that you actually read my book. I love you. Thanks, honey.*

What
Rather self-explanatory. I imagine you have probably used this sign without even realizing it.

☐ I know this sign
☐ My dog knows this sign

American Sign Language Dictionary

Where
Shake your index finger back and forth.

☐ I know this sign
☐ My dog knows this sign

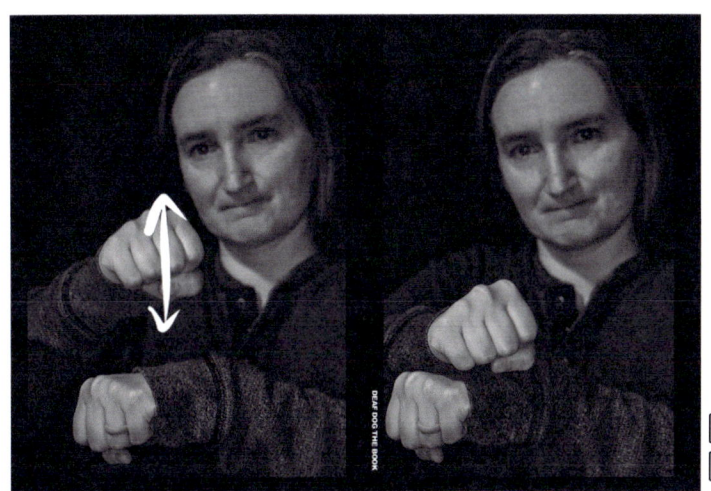

Work
Pound your two fists together as if you are hammering.

☐ I know this sign
☐ My dog knows this sign

Wrong
Using your face to express your tone, sign this to your dog to ask, "What's wrong?"

Your expression is your tone of voice.

☐ I know this sign
☐ My dog knows this sign

American Sign Language Dictionary

Yes
Move your fist up and down as if you are nodding your head.

Your expression is your tone of voice.

☐ I know this sign
☐ My dog knows this sign

You
If no one has ever told you this before, "You CAN do it."

Of course, there is no way that I can include every word that every family will need. When you find that you need to expand your ASL vocabulary, simply ask Google. There is this neat video that will typically show up in most browsers.

☐ I know this sign
☐ My dog knows this sign

Do you, and your dog, know all of the signs in his book?

Way to go!

You can now brag to everyone that you are fluent in Dog Sign Language!

Let us know! #fluentDSL

I'm fluent in DSL!

Dog Sign Language.

DEAF DOG

GET YOUR BEARDED DRAGON A WIG!
Made from 100% Organic River Hair

Not really.
Don't be bugging me about this mess.

DEAF DOG 115

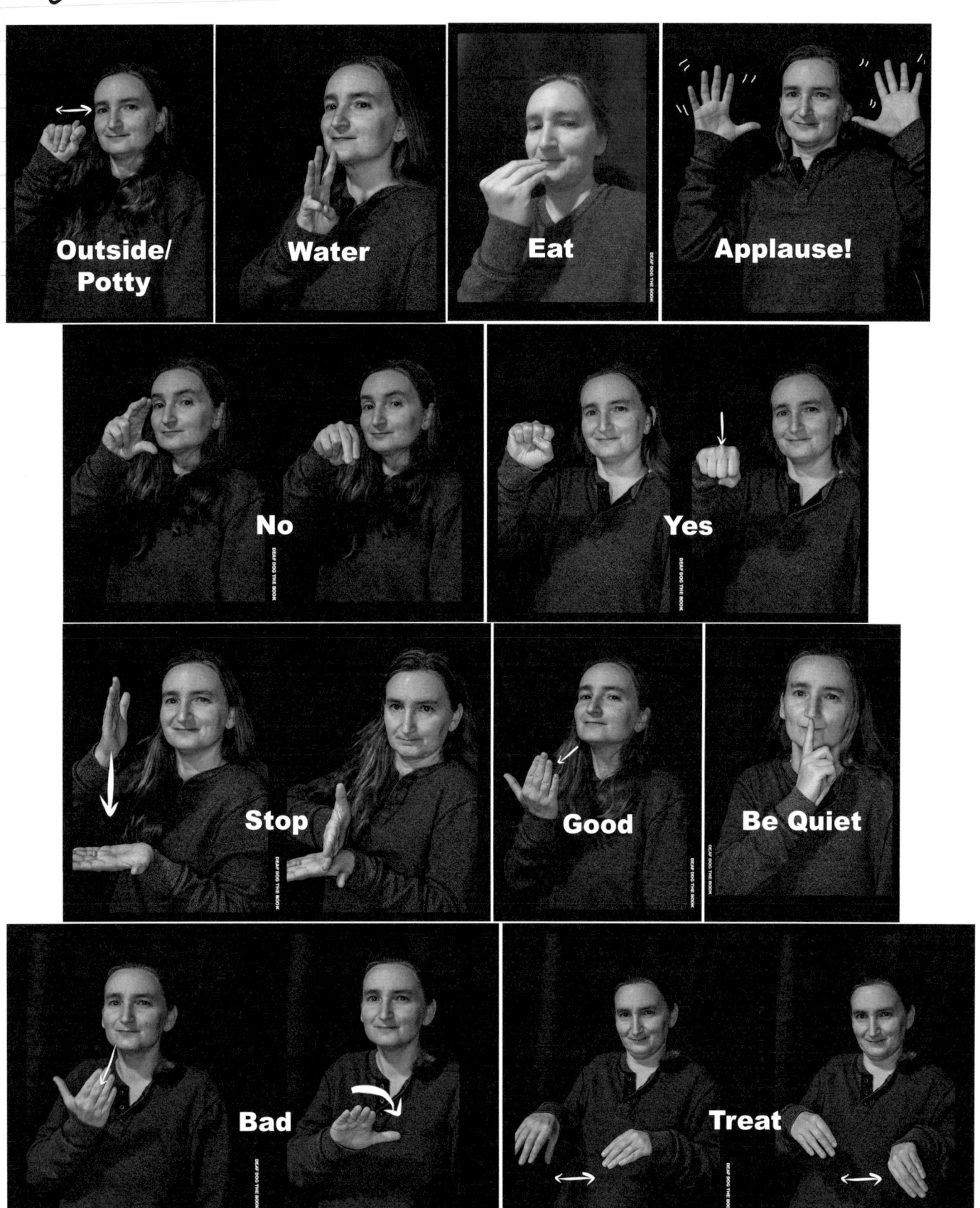

Dog's Name: _____   Quick Reference Sheet

Outside/Potty	Water	Eat	Applause!

No	Yes

Stop	Good	Be Quiet

Bad	Treat

DEAF DOG

This page is left blank 'cause it's the back of the poster!

As my grandmother used to say, "We'll be stronger on the other side of every struggle."

Dog's Name: _____   Quick Reference Sheet

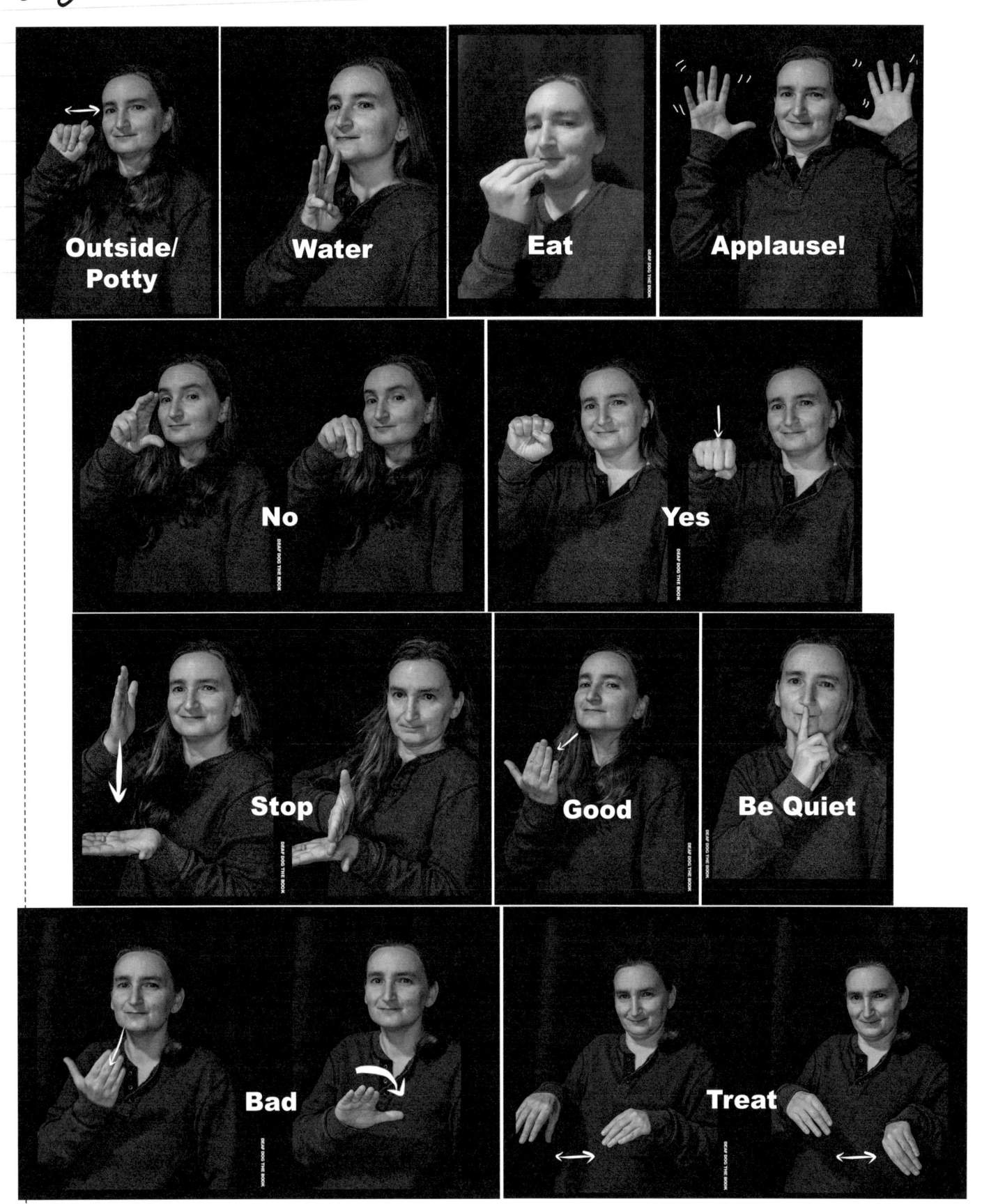

| Outside/Potty | Water | Eat | Applause! |

| No | Yes |

| Stop | Good | Be Quiet |

| Bad | Treat |

DEAF DOG 119

This page is left blank 'cause it's the back of the poster!

More advice from my grandmother...
"Everyone makes decisions based on the information they have at the time.
Later, we often gather more information and become angry with ourselves for making the wrong decision.
Don't.
Realize that you made the BEST decision you could at the time.
Move on. "

Dog's Name: _____   Quick Reference Sheet

Outside/Potty	Water
Eat	Applause!
No	Yes
Stop	Good
Be Quiet	Bad
Treat	

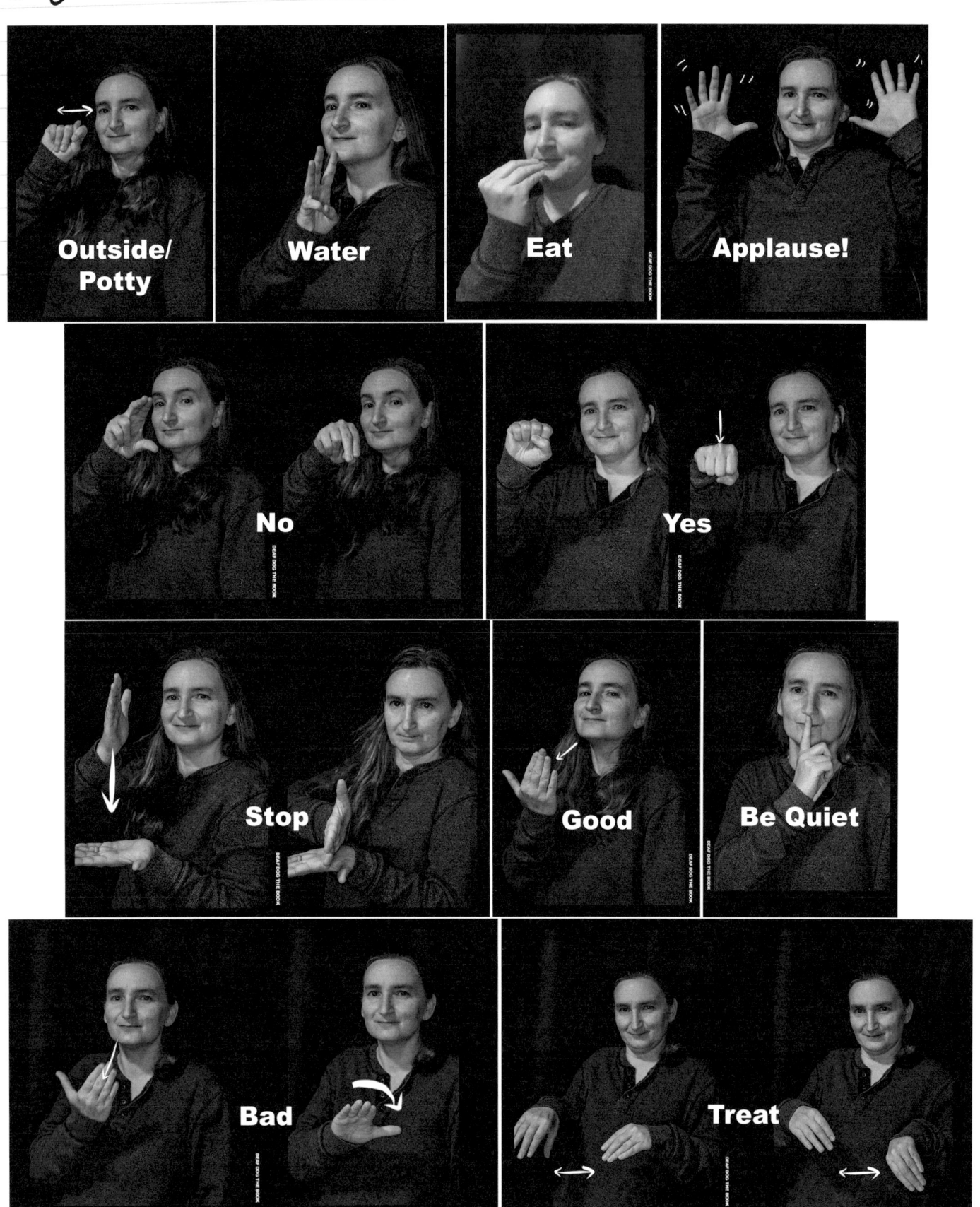

DEAF DOG 121

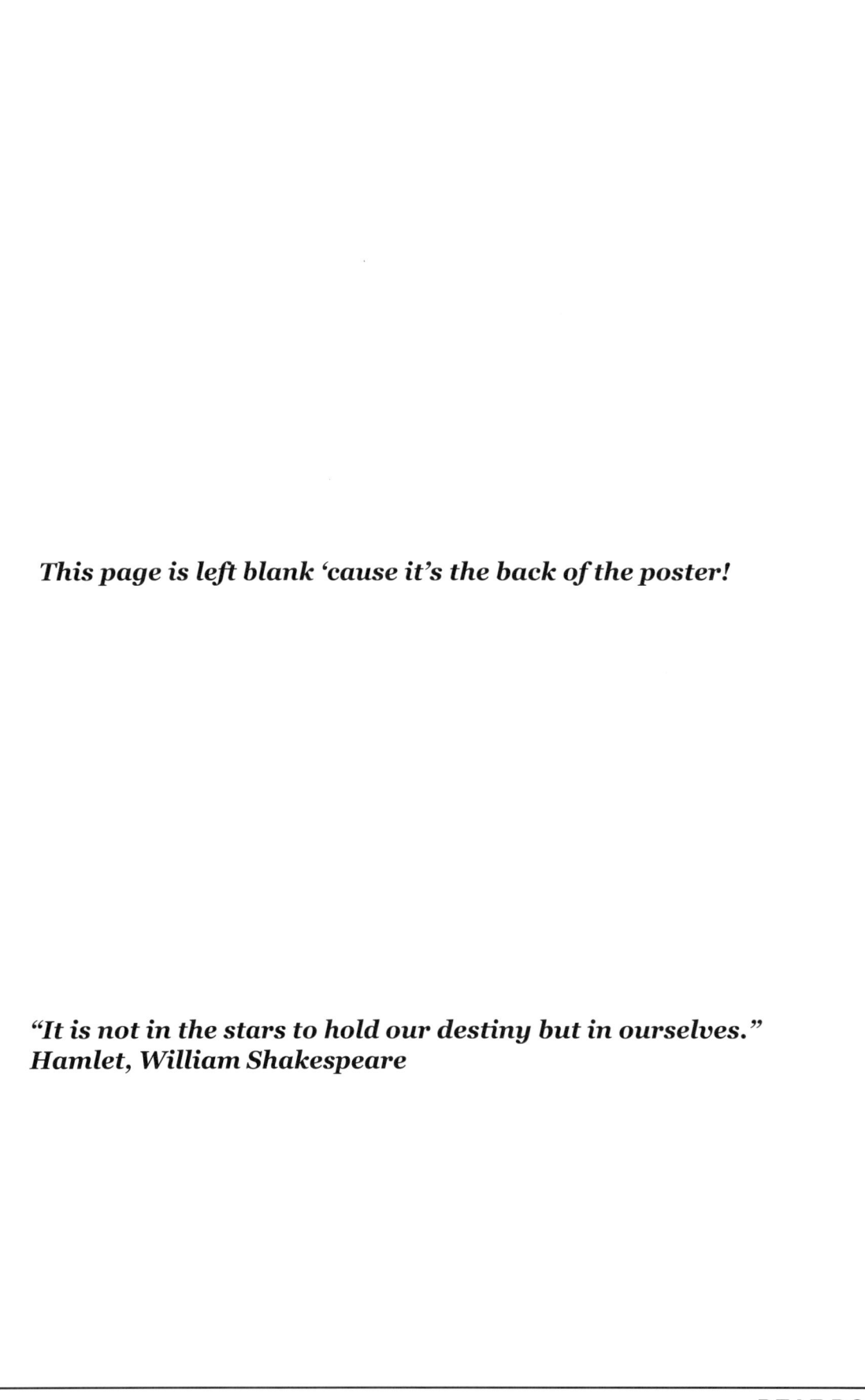

This page is left blank 'cause it's the back of the poster!

"It is not in the stars to hold our destiny but in ourselves."
Hamlet, William Shakespeare

Thank you for purchasing and reading our book. It was the collective effort of our small family to produce it for you. The more awareness we bring to how amazing a deaf pet can be, more of them will be saved and adopted into loving homes.

If you enjoyed this book, could we please ask you to go to Amazon and leave a review?

Reviews are how books like ours (self-published) get higher in the rankings. The higher we get, the more books we have the opportunity to sell.

It has been our honor to donate numerous free digital copies of this book to new families who have just adopted their first deaf dog. We're so happy to have helped them build the foundation that will help them communicate with their dog and offer them a happier life.

Think of someone you know who may enjoy our book and recommend it to them.

A dog lover?

Your veterinarian?

A dog trainer?

The neighbor that helps with your pets when you go out of town?

Your extended family who will be around your dog?

A child who has an interest in sign language?

An adult who has just discovered their dog may be losing their hearing?

For a list of additional resources, see our website www.deafdogthebook.com

Other books by Christi Bender

Grampy and Ginny introduce us to scrapbooking index cards! Grampy has always organized his day using this simple technique that he will explain to you, while Ginny helps you make them "beau-ti-mus!"

Instructions along with ready-made images for you to color and cut out, or maybe copy them for a larger group.

A portion of this book benefits Advocates for Children.

Now available!

An Artist's Sketchbook
Black and White Sketches for Inspiration or Coloring

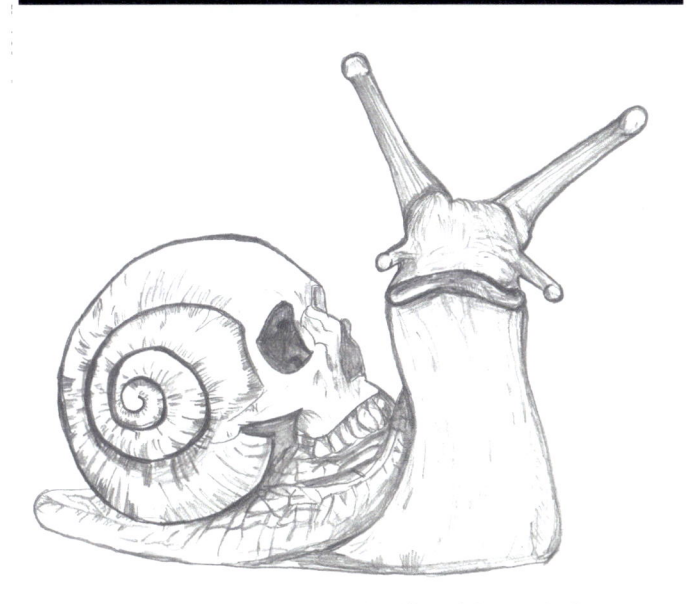

Ever wanted to look inside an artist's sketchbook? Here's your chance!

Artist Christi Bender has gathered some of her favorite sketches together along with some advice for the beginning artist.

All sketches have been taken directly out of the sketchbooks and most have shading already applied.

Fancy coloring in the images?

Grab some colored pencils or crayons and go for it! Available on Amazon

DEAF DOG

Made in United States
Troutdale, OR
04/08/2025